People's Republic of China

People's Republic of China

BY KIM DRAMER

Enchantment of the World
Second Series

Children's Press®

A Division of Grolier Publishing

NEW YORK   LONDON   HONG KONG   SYDNEY
DANBURY, CONNECTICUT

Frontispiece: Chinese opera performer in full costume

Consultant: Heather Colburn, Ph.D. candidate, Department of Art History and
Archaeology, Columbia University, and Project Associate, Education
Division, Asia Society

Please note: All statistics are as up-to-date as possible at the time of publication.

Visit Children's Press on the Internet: http://publishing.grolier.com

Book production: Herman Adler Design Group

Library of Congress Cataloging-in-Publication Data

Dramer, Kim.
    People's Republic of China / by Kim Dramer.
        p. cm. — (Enchantment of the world. Second series)
    Includes bibliographical references and index.
    Summary: Describes the geography, plants and animals, history,
economy, language, religions, culture, and people of the People's
Republic of China, home of one of the world's oldest continuous
civilizations.
    ISBN 0-516-21077-7
    1. China—Juvenile literature. [1. China.] I. Title.
II. Series.
DS706.D73 1999
915.1—dc21   98-17643
                                                                              CIP
                                                                               AC

People's Republic of China

Contents

Cover photo:
The Great Wall
of China

A family from Guizhou

Chinese porcelain

The Center of the World

The Chinese call their country the Middle Kingdom. The name shows how the Chinese feel about the importance of China on the face of the globe.

CHINA'S EARLIEST HISTORY IS SHROUDED IN THE LEGEND of the Five Sovereigns. These are mythical kings of China's prehistory. The Five Sovereigns are said to have taught the Chinese people hunting, fishing, raising animals, and agriculture. They also established the institutions of marriage and family.

Today, historians view China as the world's oldest continuous civilization. Chinese history has always been dynamic, with great cultural developments and changes. Yet the customs and traditions that define China have remained relatively unchanged. These include the standardized written language, geographical features, and Confucian-based systems of government that helped China to repeatedly strengthen its cultural system.

Opposite: **Sea of Wisdom Temple on Longevity Hill, Beijing**

China

The Chinese characters for *China* show the Chinese people's view of their country's role in the world. The meaning of the character on the left, *middle*, can be seen from its structure. The character on the right, *kingdom*, shows the borders of the territory surrounding a spear used in their defense.

Geopolitical map of
the People's Republic
of China

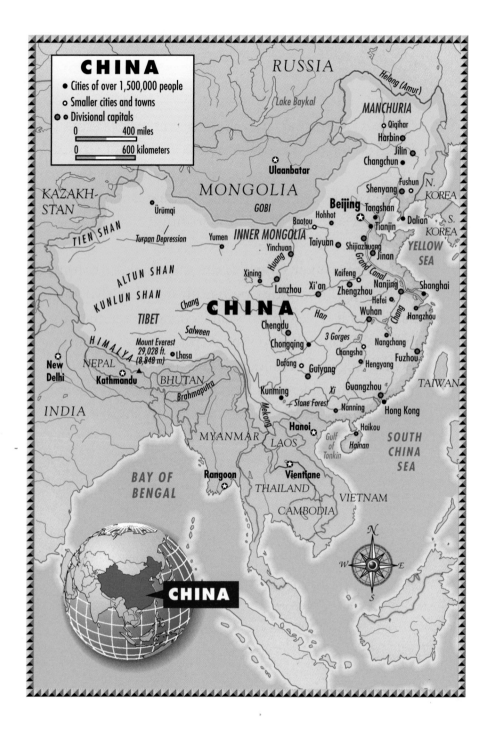

The Chinese Empire was formed in 221 B.C., when seven "Warring States" ruled by feudal lords were united by a conqueror from the State of Qin named Shi Huangdi. This man called himself the emperor, or Son of Heaven—a title used by all the rulers of Imperial China until the twentieth century.

The first emperor united China with a series of reforms and a massive building campaign. He standardized the weights and measures used in trade. He also standardized written Chinese characters so that people speaking different dialects throughout China could understand one another. That system of writing was much the same as the system the Chinese use today. The written link between China's past and present is unique in the world.

The first emperor built a huge tomb for himself, guarded by thousands of clay soldiers. And he linked a series of ancient defensive walls. These are thought to be the beginning of the Great Wall, the most ancient and enduring symbol of China.

After the Qin, China was ruled by successive dynasties—emperors belonging to the same family. The Chinese believed that each emperor ruled China through heaven's approval. This was called the "Mandate of Heaven," an agreement among the emperor, his subjects, and his heavenly ancestors.

This system of rule ensured lengthy and relatively peaceful dynasties for more than 2,000 years. During that period, Chinese people made many great scientific and technological advances and achieved artistic greatness in literature and the fine arts.

Today, China is the world's most populous nation. It is poised as an emerging world superpower, but it is aware of its past glory and the value of its traditional arts. In 1998, president Bill Clinton of the United States toured the Great Wall with President Jiang Zemin of China. Speaking on Chinese television, President Clinton expressed the importance of appreciating China's historical greatness while understanding China's role today as a superpower.

Today's Chinese people and their leaders are working hard to reestablish China's national security and prosperity. At the same time, the preservation of Chinese traditional culture is an important goal of the country. Their efforts are designed to ensure China's status as the world's true Middle Kingdom.

Opposite: **Life-size terra cotta figures of the Lishan Mausoleum, the tomb of the first emperor**

Visitors relaxing in the Long Corridor of the Summer Palace in Beijing

A Land of Contrasts

China's landscape as well as its people have been in a state of continual change throughout history. Today's map of the People's Republic of China is the product of the modern union of different cultural, ethnic, geographical, and historic spheres.

THE MAIN CHANGE IN THE MAP IS THE UNITY OF INNER China with the borderlands of north and west China, known as Outer China. For most of China's history, these two regions were quite separate.

Opposite: **A man on a water buffalo overlooking terraced rice fields in Yunnan province**

Inner China

Inner China is a low-lying area of heavily cultivated land. The productive farmland of the region is reflected in its dense population and its complex network of transportation. Roads, rail, and water transportation link the *Chang* (Yangze) River and the *Huanghe* (Yellow River) with the eastern coast.

A busy shopping street in Shanghai

The Great Wall

The human-made structure that marks the traditional border between Inner and Outer China is known as the Great Wall. It is about 1,500 miles (2,414 kilometers) long. Its enormous scale makes the Great Wall the only human-made structure that is visible from the moon.

Most of what we call the Great Wall today was built during the Ming dynasty in the late fifteenth century. The Ming dynasty ruled from 1368 to 1644. These walls are visited by thousands of tourists each year.

Ancient Chinese people began building *changcheng* (long walls) in the fourth century B.C., but few traces of these earthen walls remain. The Chinese word for city comes from the word *cheng*, meaning "wall," because the ancient Chinese surrounded their cities with earthen walls.

The Great Wall was begun in the third century B.C. when the first emperor joined a series of walls built by the previous warring states. These walls had been used to keep out invaders from the north and to launch attacks into that area.

The first emperor used war prisoners and criminals to link these walls. When the work was too slow, he ordered Chinese farmers to leave their fields and help complete the project. The workers often went hungry and toiled in the bitter winter without warm clothing. When a worker died, the body was often thrown into the structure and covered with bricks. The Great Wall thus became a symbol of oppression and inhumanity as well as of the might of the emperor.

Traditional historians view the Great Wall as a symbol of China's power. However, Communist historians concentrate on the story of the ordinary men and women whose forced labor built the Great Wall.

For most Chinese people, the Great Wall is a source of pride and an important part of China's identity. It is a symbol of the nation's civilization and patriotism. The Chinese point to the work of the ordinary Chinese men and women who labored to build the wall. At the same time, they know that the Great Wall is a symbol of China's historic military strength.

Outer China

Outer China, or frontier China, is an area of geographical extremes and spectacular scenery. It is home to the world's highest mountain, *Qomolangma* (Mount Everest), some 29,028 feet (8,848 m) above sea level. China's lowest point, also located in Outer China, is the Turpan Depression in Xinjiang Autonomous Region, some 505 feet (154 m) below sea level.

A mountaineer on the ridge-top of Qomolangma, or Mount Everest, the world's highest mountain

Looking at Chinese Cities

China's largest city is Shanghai (below), with a population of more than 13 million people. The name *Shanghai*, which means "upon the sea," refers to the city's importance as a harbor on China's eastern coast. Shanghai began as a fishing village. During the nineteenth century, it was a major trading port for foreign powers. Today, the city is a center of manufacturing, trade, and banking. It retains its European flavor and important place in international commerce. Shanghai residents enjoy an average January temperature of 39° Fahrenheit (4° Celcius) and an average July temperature of 82°F (28°C).

Guangzhou, southern China's major port and city, was founded by the first Qin emperor in 214 B.C. Until 1842, it was the only Chinese port open to foreign trade. Guangzhou's coldest January temperature is about 32°F (0°C), and its hottest July temperature is about 100°F (38°C).

Shenyang, in northeastern China, was founded about A.D. 1000. It served as the Manchu capital until 1644. Today, Shenyang is a major industrial city, producing machinery, aircraft, and rubber goods. The city's residents have Manchu, Han Chinese, Korean, and Russian ancestors.

Tianjin is a major northern China port and industrial city. It is the political and historical center of southern Manchuria. High-quality bicycles and watches made in Tianjin are sold throughout China.

Historically, Outer China was cut off from Inner China by dangerous terrain or impassable areas. The famous Silk Routes were a complex network of trade routes linking China to the Middle East, Europe, and India via a series of oases. Over the centuries, both trade goods and ideas traveled along the Silk Routes. China's silk, tea, and porcelains were transported by camel caravan. Traders brought ideas such as Buddhism along the routes with them. These new ideas made their way into the culture of Inner China.

A Uygur man at his fabric store in Xinjiang Province. The Silk Routes ran through oases and towns in today's Xinjiang.

A Land of Contrasts **19**

Geographical Features

Area: 3,696,100 square miles (9,572,900 sq km); the world's third-largest country after Russia and Canada.

Largest City: Shanghai, 13,584,000 people (1995 est.)

Highest Elevation: *Qomolangma* (Mount Everest) on the China-Nepal border, 29,028 feet (8,848 m) above sea level; the world's highest point

Lowest Elevation: Turfan Depression in Xinjiang, 505 feet (154 m) below sea level

Longest River: Chang (Yangtze), 3,964 (6,379 km); the world's third-longest river, after the Nile and the Amazon.

Largest Lake: Qinghai in Qinghai Province, 1,625 square miles (4,209 sq km)

Largest Desert: Gobi Desert, 500,000 square miles (1,295,000 sq km), on the China-Mongolia border; the world's second-largest desert after Africa's Sahara

Lowest Average Temperature: −22°F (−30°C) in January in northern China

Highest Average Temperature: 83° F (28°C) in July in southeastern China

Only Human-Made Structure Visible from the Moon: Great Wall of China, about 1,500 miles (2,414 km) long, 20–50 feet (6–15 m) high, and 15–25 feet (5–8 m) thick; the world's longest human-made structure

Qomolangma

The highest point on earth, majestic Qomolangma (Mount Everest) rises on the border of Nepal and Tibet in China. Local people call it the Goddess Mother of the World. The mountain's English name honors Sir George Everest, a British surveyor-general of India in the 1800s.

Qomolangma rises two-thirds of the way through Earth's atmosphere. Here, oxygen levels are low, temperatures are cold, and winds are powerful. Because of these extremes, the mountain has no plant or animal life. The peak of Qomolangma was first conquered in 1953.

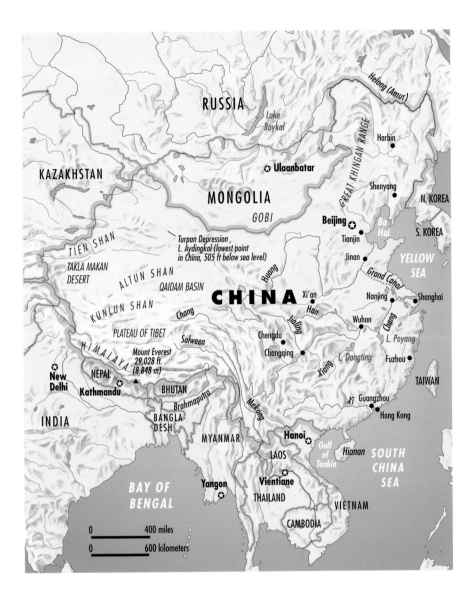

Inner and Outer China are land masses of comparable size, but Outer China is home to only 5 percent of the country's population. Outer China's frontier areas are the homeland of many of China's ethnic minorities.

Internal Divisions

Province	Municipality	Autonomous Region

1	Anhui	10	Henan	19	Qinghai
2	Fujian	11	Hubei	20	Shaanxi
3	Gansu	12	Hunan	21	Shandong
4	Guangdong	13	Jiangsu	22	Shanxi
5	Guangxi Zhuangzu	14	Jiangxi	23	Sichuan
6	Guizhou	15	Jilin	24	Xinjiang Uygur
7	Hainan	16	Liaoning	25	Xizang(Tibet)
8	Hebei	17	Nei Monggol	26	Yunnan
9	Heilongjiang	18	Ningxia Huizu	27	Zhejiang

When Inner and Outer China were united during the Qing dynasty (1644–1911), China's area became only slightly larger than that of the United States. The current map of China reflects the historic division of the two regions by the presence of Autonomous Regions including Inner Mongolia, Xinjiang, Ningxia, Guangxi, and Tibet.

Climate

Because China is spread out over such an immense area and has such a varied landscape, its weather includes extremes from bitter cold to unbearable heat. China's climate follows a general pattern of change from tropical to moderate in the southeast through a cooler middle belt, ending in arid and high-mountain climates in the northwest.

The hottest spot in China is Turfan, located in a depression in Xinjiang. Temperatures in summer may soar to 116°F (47°C), but can drop to –22°F(–30°C) in winter.

Tibet has a unique climate due to its high altitude and thin air. Winters here are endless days and nights of piercing, dry cold. Summers are warm and dry, but weather can quickly change in the thin air.

China North and South

Inner China is divided into north and south. The area to the north is dominated by the Yellow River. The south is dominated by the Yangze River.

The Yellow River gets its name from the yellow silt it carries in its waters. This silt, called loess, is a very fine sand, blown by the prevailing winds from the Gobi Desert in the west. Over thousands of years, deposits of loess that are hundreds of feet

The Yellow River

deep have accumulated over the central plain of northern China. As the Yellow River cuts through this layer of loess, its waters become yellow.

The silt in the riverbed has also caused the terrible flooding that gives the Yellow River the name "China's Sorrow." Over the centuries, the Chinese have built dikes to control the waters. The dikes are so high in certain sections that the river water actually flows above the lands that border it.

The waters of the Yangze River are more stable. The Yangze's water flow is regulated by two great lakes in middle

The construction of the Three Gorges Hydroelectric Dam

Three Gorges

The building of the Three Gorges Hydroelectric Dam has been called China's most ambitious project since the Great Wall. It is slated for completion in 2009.

Designed to regulate the waters of the Yangze River, whose devastating floods have claimed more than 300,000 lives in the 1900s alone, the reservoir will have a system of locks to allow shipping and bring prosperity to the region. The dam will be the most powerful ever built.

Many experts have pointed to the project's ecological dangers. Others have lamented the destruc-tion of valuable archaeological sites that may hold clues to the origins of Chinese civilization. Nearly 2 million people will have to leave their homes in more than one thousand towns and villages along the waterway.

Also affected by the rising level of the newly har-nessed waters will be the famous Three Gorges (above). Chinese literature has many poems and stories about these towering limestone cliffs. They form a 200-mile (322-km) canyon along the Yangze—one of China's scenic wonders.

course—the Dongting and the Poyang. These lakes act as reservoirs in times of drought and provide overflow basins to prevent flooding.

The Chinese government has started the construction of the world's largest dam on the Yangze at the site of the Three Gorges. The dam is designed to harvest the power of the river for hydroelectric projects and to control flooding. If the government succeeds in this monumental project, great benefits will come to people of the region. However, many experts have expressed fears that the project will fail.

The Grand Canal

Over the centuries, the Chinese built a series of canals to link the Yellow River in the north to the Yangze River in the south. The most important part of this system is the Grand Canal.

The Grand Canal begins in Beijing and ends in Hangzhou, linking the Hai, Yellow, Yangze, and Qiantang Rivers. The Grand Canal differs from these natural rivers because it flows from north to south.

The Grand Canal is the oldest and longest human-made waterway in the world. Its construction took 1,779 years—from 486 B.C. to A.D. 1293. The canal is 1,115 miles (1,794 km) long. Like the Great Wall, it stands as a magnificent achievement of ancient China. It too was constructed with forced labor, including female workers.

During times of famine, the Grand Canal was the lifeline that brought surplus grain from the south to needy people in the north. The canal also made it easier to collect taxes, distribute grain, and transport soldiers.

Before parts of it silted up over the last century, the Grand Canal provided irrigation to surrounding farmers. It also helped develop economic and cultural ties between northern and southern China.

The Coastline

China's coastline extends more than 11,185 miles (18,000 km), from the mouth of the Yalu River in the north to the mouth of the Beilun River on the China-Vietnam border in the south. The Chinese mainland borders three sea areas—the Yellow Sea, the East China Sea, and the South China Sea—in addition to the Bo Hai Sea, an inland sea of China. The South China Sea has the features and depth of an ocean basin. The others are mostly shallow continental shelves, suitable for the development of fish farms. The continental shelves also contain oil deposits that are of great importance to China's national economy.

China has more than 5,000 coastal islands. The vast majority of these islands are scattered in the coastal waters south of Hangzhou Bay and the South China Sea.

Taiwan, China's largest island, has a democratic form of government that is separate from the People's Republic of China. The largest island under China's jurisdiction is Hainan Island in the South China Sea. This large island grows tropical products including coconuts and tea. There is also a major submarine base on Hainan Island to defend China's coast.

From Silkworm to Dragon

The *long* (dragon) is the animal associated with traditional China and imperial rule. The Chinese dragon is a mythical beast made up of seven animals. Ancient Chinese texts describe the dragon as having the head of a camel, the scales of a fish, the horns of a deer, the claws of an eagle, the whiskers of a cat, the ears of a bull, and the eyes of a demon.

A dragon in a New Year's parade

Tʜɪs Cʜɪɴᴇsᴇ ᴅʀᴀɢᴏɴ ᴄᴀɴ ᴄʜᴀɴɢᴇ ɪᴛs sɪᴢᴇ ᴀᴛ ᴡɪʟʟ. It can become as small as a silkworm or large enough to cast a shadow over the entire earth.

However, the Chinese dragon is not the fire-breathing monster of Western fable. It is a gentle creature. The dragon brings the life-giving rain clouds of spring that enable Chinese farmers to grow their crops after the long winter.

Opposite: **A bronze tortoise in the Forbidden City, Beijing**

Dragon Bones

Farmers in the Yellow River Valley in northern China often found bones with strange carvings on them. The farmers called them "dragon bones," believing them to come from mythical creatures.

The local Chinese believed these bones had special healing powers. Dragon bones were sold to the local pharmacy, where they were used to make traditional Chinese medicine.

Chinese scholars realized that the strange carvings on the bones were an ancient system of writing. In China's first official archaeological dig, thousands of these bones were unearthed at Anyang. The characters were carved on the backbones of oxen as well as on a number of turtle shells. Archaeologists called the writing *jia gu wen* (bone-shell writing). About 2,000 characters of this ancient written language have been recorded. Of these, about half have been deciphered.

The carvings are from the Shang Dynasty (about 1766 B.C.–A.D. 1059). They are questions from the Shang king to his ancestors regarding harvests, weather, hunting, and the birth of sons. In return, the Shang king offers elaborate sacrifices, including the sacrifice of humans, to honor the ancestors' spirits.

China's New Ambassador

In today's world, the giant panda is the animal most people associate with China. Called *xiongmao* (bear-cats) by the Chinese, the panda is China's ambassador to the world. The two pandas in the National Zoo in Washington, D.C., were gifts from China.

Fossils of pandas date back more than half a million years. Today, fewer than one thousand pandas survive.

The panda is one of the world's most specialized animals. Pandas feed almost exclusively on bamboo. They live deep in the mountains of China to the south and north of the Yangze River, where the local forests can support their limited diet.

Bamboo follows a natural cycle of death and regrowth as it flowers and reseeds itself. This cycle ranges from several years to one hundred years. When the bamboo in an area dies, the pandas who live there face starvation.

A giant panda eating bamboo

Today, worldwide efforts are underway to save this endangered species. Scientists have conducted studies of the panda's breeding habits and have begun efforts to breed pandas in captivity.

Environmentalists have established protected areas for pandas within China. The Wolong Nature Reserve, supported by the World Wildlife Fund, is the largest area dedicated to preserving this unique species. The World Wildlife Fund has chosen the panda as its symbol.

Relict Species

The panda is just one example of so-called relict species of plants and animals in China. These are species that survived the Ice Age in protected niches of the environment. The dawn redwood, the only living relative of the famous California redwoods, is the most famous relict plant in China.

The ginkgo tree is another relict plant native to China. The ginkgo is the only remaining species of a group of trees widely distributed in prehistoric times. The hardy ginkgo is often used in city landscapes in North America, where it can withstand the rigors of urban pollution.

The ginkgo grows to 100 feet (30 m) tall and 3 feet (91 cm) in diameter. It has fan-shaped leaves and a plumlike fruit with thin, pulpy flesh and a large white seed. The fruit gives off a foul odor as it decomposes.

Chinese harvest the seeds for eating. One Chinese dessert is a dish of ginkgo seeds in burnt sugar sauce. This dish is called "Poetry and Rite Silver Ginkgo," after the ginkgo tree under which Confucius taught.

A National Flower

China's national flower is the splendid and fragrant peony. Formerly, China was called the *hua gua* (flowery kingdom). The Chinese chose the splendid peony, hardy yet fragrant, as a symbol of China's past glories and future hopes.

Cultivated Plants

China is also home to many wild species of commonly cultivated plants, such as oranges, chestnuts, rice, and walnuts. Many flowers, trees, and fruits we see in North

Three Friends of Winter

Chinese people have found rich symbolism in the plants of the country to express their ideals and hopes. Most famous among these are the "Three Friends of Winter"—bamboo, plum blossom, and pine.

The bamboo is treasured for its ability to bend with the wind yet remain upright and straight. Its hollow stem is "impartial" and thus free of prejudice and judgment. For this reason, it symbolizes strength and everlasting friendship. The winter plum blossom symbolizes personal renewal and political unrest. It is the first flower to blossom each spring. The pine tree's ability to withstand the rigors of frost symbolizes inner strength and longevity.

The Three Friends of Winter have come to symbolize the qualities needed in the face of hardship. They are often painted together in Chinese art. So what may appear to be a charming still life painting to a Westerner is actually a moral statement about how to live life to a Chinese.

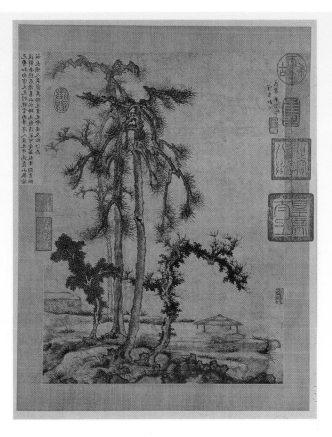

America originated in China. The orange, the rhododendron, the tea rose, the dahlia, and the kiwi fruit all came from China.

Buddhist Plants

The lotus flower is a symbol of Buddhism. The wild aquatic lotus plant, with its large pink flowers, flourishes in China's swamps and marshes. The lotus grows through the muddy water that symbolizes the mundane world to emerge clean and perfect in the light. For this reason, it symbolizes the Buddha's wisdom and enlightenment. He, too, was uncorrupted by the tainted world about him and by the temptations of everyday life. Many Buddhist statues and porcelain pieces feature the lotus.

Another plant associated with Buddhism is the *bodhi* (pipal) tree. Devout Buddhists believe that the Buddha meditated under the branches of this tree at Bodhgaya when he became enlightened. Seedlings from that sacred tree were carried all over the Buddhist world to be planted and worshiped.

Tea, an indispensable part of the life of the Chinese, is associated with the Buddhist monk Lu Yu. Lu, who lived during the Tang dynasty (A.D. 618–907), helped popularize tea drinking all across China, making tea drinkers of everyone from emperor to farmer.

Tea is made from the leaves of the tea tree. Different methods of processing the leaves result in different kinds of tea. Various tastes, colors, and fragrances depend on the way the leaves are fermented and roasted. Tea that has not been fermented is called green tea.

The Chinese believe that tea is beneficial to health by improving eyesight and increasing alertness. They consider tea to be a natural health food.

In the early seventeenth century, the Dutch East India Company introduced Chinese tea to England. Soon, afternoon tea had become a ritual for British nobility and made its way across the Atlantic to North America.

Lacquer

The *lac*, or varnish, tree is found in the midstream and basin areas of the Yellow River. The sap of these trees is known for its strong adhesive quality and beautiful gloss. This sap is called lacquer. Chinese discovered early on that lacquer could be used as a protective adhesive and beautifying agent. As early as the Neolithic Age, the Chinese knew how to use lacquer to decorate ornaments and ritual objects.

Lacquerware is made by brushing layers of the lacquer onto an object, often carved of wood. As the layers are built up, the object takes on a smooth, brilliant finish. The lacquer may be carved, gilded, or painted for a variety of surface effects.

Conservation Efforts

Some of the world's rarest deer, wild horses, mountain sheep, and wild cats are also found in China. Many of these animals live in the harsh terrain of Outer China.

Przewalski's horse is the last true wild horse. These horses are at a research and breeding station in Xinjiang.

The Chinese alligator is now an endangered animal and a focus of conservation efforts. There are more species of tiger in China than in any other country. China's Manchurian, or Siberian, tiger is the world's largest tiger. The tiger is the king of beasts for the Chinese. Many Chinese folktales tell about heroes who fight and overcome ferocious tigers.

The Chinese recognize that all these animals are national treasures. They have worked to preserve China's rich wildlife by establishing a network of nature reserves. By 2000, China will have more than 500 such reserves.

The snow leopard is rare and endangered.

Tigers are one type of wild cat that lives in China.

Traditional Chinese Medicine

Some Chinese conservation efforts are in direct conflict with traditional Chinese culture and the idea that many of these animals possess the power to cure illness in humans. Traditional Chinese prescriptions often consist of plants and animals boiled together into a soup or tea. For example, a Chinese prescription might include bear liver to treat a person whose own liver function is impaired.

Ginseng is a plant believed by many East Asians to be a general tonic, good for keeping the body healthy. The root of the ginseng is said to resemble the figure of the human body. Chinese harvest the root from both wild and cultivated ginseng plants.

Herbs used in traditional Chinese medicine

The Yeti

Another unique species is rumored to exist in China but has proved elusive to scientists. The yeti has been the subject of intense scientific investigation. The yeti is a humanlike creature said to live in the harsh terrain of the Himalaya region in Tibet. Sherpas, natives of the Himalayan countries of Bhutan and Nepal and of Tibet, have long believed in the existence of wild men who wander the northern mountain areas.

The Chinese call this creature *Yen ren* (wild man). The popular English name for the creature is "Abominable Snowman."

There is still no definite proof of the yeti's existence, but sightings of the creature and the discovery of huge footprints have been reported. The footprints look much like those of a barefoot human, but they are wider and shorter. They have five toes, but three of them seem to have claws.

The creature is described as 6 to 7 feet (1.8 to 2 m) tall, walking upright, and covered with long, dark hair. It is said to have an eerie, high-pitched cry.

The yeti may be a type of ape that is still unclassified, a remainder of Neanderthal man—or merely a myth. China has sponsored several scientific expeditions to find a yeti, but without success so far.

Silkworms on leaf-filled trays

Silk

The manufacture of silk has been a hallmark of Chinese civilization for 5,000 years. Silk manufacture depends on the combination of an animal and a plant—the silkworm and the mulberry tree. The silkworm feeds exclusively upon mulberry leaves. Each spring, these leaves are harvested to feed silkworms raised in captivity. This was traditionally the work of women, who pick the leaves from trees 50 to 70 feet (15 to 21 m) high.

The silkworms spin a cocoon from a single strand of thread between 2,000 and 3,000 feet (610 and 914 m) long. These cocoons are soaked, steamed, and unwound to recover the silk strand. Several strands of silk are then combined to make a thread.

Silk making was a jealously guarded secret for centuries. One legend says that the secret of silk making was smuggled out of China by a princess. Commanded to marry a foreign prince in the West, she hid silk cocoons in an elaborate headdress she wore as she left China for her new home.

A worker manufacturing silk inside a silk factory

Bactrian Camels

The Silk Routes divided into a northern and a southern caravan route around the Takla Makan Desert. Along these routes, men carried both products and ideas. The two-humped Bactrian camel made it possible to travel over long stretches of desert. On these camels, missionaries and travelers journeyed between China, Central Asia, India, and Europe.

Bactrian camels carried people as well as heavy loads. Their ability to walk and run over desert sands made them valuable. They could also sniff out underwater springs and predict deadly sandstorms.

The Chinese obtained these camels in various ways. Some were bought, some were given, and some were taken in

Bactrian camels in the Gobi Desert

wars. Many pottery models of these beasts from the Tang dynasty (618–907) are found in Western museums. These are usually fashioned of hollow clay made from molds and coated with brown, green, and creamy yellow glazing called "three-color ware."

Dogs

Many kinds of dogs familiar in North America came from China. The Pekingese used to be known as "sleeve dogs" because the tiny, short-legged breed could be carried in the long, flowing sleeves of wealthy Chinese. The shih tzu, developed in Beijing during the 1600s, was a great favorite of the emperors of China.

Working dogs from China include the chow chow and the shar-pei. The chow chow has been popular in China for at least 2,000 years. It is big enough to be used as a guard dog and strong enough to pull carts. The shar-pei is known for the folds of loose skin covering its body, especially its head. It was developed for dogfighting, a popular sport in the 1500s, because its loose skin made it impossible to pin down in a dogfight.

The geographic isolation of Tibet led to the breeding of distinctive types of dog. The Tibetan spaniel was a companion of Buddhist monks in the monasteries of Tibet. It is said to have turned the prayer wheels for the praying monks. The Lhasa apso is another dog associated with Tibetan Buddhism. The present of a Lhasa apso was a traditional gift of the Dalai Lama, a Tibetan spiritual leader. The Tibetan mastiff is a large dog that can weigh up to 180 pounds (82 kg). It was originally bred for guarding flocks in the mountains of Tibet.

A child sitting on a yak in Tibet being led by her mother

Tibet is home to a population of seminomadic people who raise goats, sheep, and yaks. The hardy yaks are the cattle of Tibet and an important part of Tibetan life and culture. Larger than domestic cattle, the yak has curved horns, short legs, high shoulders, and long hair hanging from its flanks, legs, and tail.

For Tibetans, the yak provides many of life's essentials. The hair of the yak is sheared and then pounded together to make a felt cloth. This cloth is used to make yurts (tents) that are naturally waterproof. The meat of the yak is eaten fresh or made into meat jerky by drying it in strips. The milk of the yak is good to drink. Sometimes it is salted and added to tea. Some yak milk is churned into butter. Some of this butter is eaten, some is burned in lamps for Tibetan Buddhist worship, and some is carved into Buddhist sculpture.

The Ta'er Lamasery, built in 1577, has a collection of yak butter sculpture depicting humans, animals, and landscapes. The art of butter sculpture probably dates back 1,300 years.

Yaks are also used to carry people and heavy loads. When a Tibetan family moves house, it packs its yak-felt tent onto the back of a yak. During the move, the family will eat yak jerky and drink tea with yak milk and salt.

Household Pets

Many Chinese children keep a cricket in a tiny cage as a summer pet. During the warm summer evenings, the chirping of a cricket is a soothing sound to which they fall asleep.

Cricket fighting is a popular amusement in China. Crickets are trained to fight and pitted against one another. Spectators often place a bet on the cricket they believe will win the fight.

Another summer pet enjoyed by Chinese children is the cicada. In North America, the cicada is often called a katydid. As the summer sun sets, the shrill song of the cicada fills the air. This sound is produced by two vibrating sheaths of skin on the abdomen of the male cicada.

The cicada has two pairs of delicate wings. It lives high up in the trees. To catch a cicada, Chinese children use a long bamboo pole with glue on one end. The child then flies the insect "airplane" on the pole. Eventually, the cicada is released.

The cicada has a fifteen-year cycle of life and death. It buries itself in the ground and emerges fifteen years later, leaving a dried skin, much like a snake. When the ancient Chinese observed this cycle of life and death, they chose the cicada as a symbol of rebirth. For this reason, one often finds images of cicada in Chinese art made for funerals.

Recently, many Chinese have begun to keep dogs as household pets. They are a great status symbol today. Ownership of dogs in cities is highly controlled and sometimes banned due to lack of space.

A People of History

The Shang dynasty was the first Chinese dynasty to leave a historical record. These records were characters carved into bones and turtle shells. They are questions asked by the Shang ruler-priest of his deceased ancestors.

ALL DECISIONS MADE BY THIS RULER WERE MADE IN collaboration with his deceased ancestors. The king consulted the ancestors by using ox bones and turtle shells in a process called divination. A question was put to the ancestors and then heated millet stalks were applied to the shells or bones until they cracked. The cracks were then read to understand the answer of the spirits. Shang kings consulted their ancestors on subjects ranging from childbirth, hunting, and warfare to the weather.

The Dynasties

The Shang were defeated by the Zhou. The Zhou was China's longest dynasty, ruling for almost 1,000 years. During this time, feudal lords battled one another. Confucius and other philosophers traveled to each court in turn, hoping to end the constant warfare. They tried to convince each lord to rule with the welfare of the people in mind rather than to expand their kingdoms by warfare. During his own lifetime, Confucius was unsuccessful at this.

China was united as a single, great empire when the lord of Qin subdued his rival feudal lords. He took the title of emperor, which was used by the ruler of every subsequent dynasty in Chinese history. This practice continued until the twentieth century.

The first Qin emperor, a warrior, disapproved of the philosophy of Confucius. Instead, he favored *legalism*, a strict

Carved bones from the late Shang dynasty

Opposite: **A glazed figure of a mounted drummer from the Tang dynasty**

Timeline of Dynasties

About 1766–1059 B.C.	Shang dynasty
1059–221	Zhou dynasty
221–206	Qin dynasty
206 B.C.–A.D. 220	Han dynasty
A.D. 581–618	Sui dynasty
618–907	Tang dynasty
907–960	Five dynasties period
960–1279	Song dynasty
1279–1368	Yuan dynasty (Mongols)
1368–1644	Ming dynasty
1644–1911	Qing dynasty (Manchus)

policy of law and order. He ordered all written records of Confucius's teachings to be destroyed. A great burning of books was ordered by the emperor. Some Chinese scholars who resisted the emperor's order were buried alive as punishment.

At the same time, the first Qin emperor began a series of great public works aimed at unifying the Chinese Empire. These included the linking of defensive walls and the construction of canals and roads. The Chinese people were forced to carry out these projects and much human misery resulted.

The Qin dynasty ended only three years after the first emperor's death when the Han dynasty was established in 206 B.C. During the Han, many of the hallmarks of Chinese imperial rule were established. Most important among these was the Imperial Examination System used to establish a civil service of bureaucrats based on merit rather than on birth.

The examination system was based on the teachings of Confucius and helped to govern China's huge population more efficiently and benevolently. The last Imperial Exams were administered during the early twentieth century.

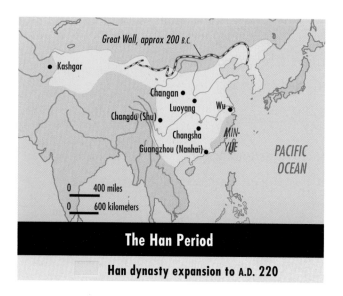

The Han Period

Han dynasty expansion to A.D. 220

Following the Han came the Period of Disunity, when the empire was divided amidst foreign domination by northern peoples. During this time, China was open to outside influences. Buddhism was added to the philosophies of Confucius and local religions.

The empire was reunified when the Sui (581–618) dynasty controlled north and south China, linking the two by building the Grand Canal. This link between the Yangze and the Yellow Rivers allowed better communications and trade. The transport of plentiful grain from the south to the north allowed the northern borders to be defended by an army.

The Tang dynasty (618–907) was a golden age for Chinese culture and is marked by extensive expansion to the west and north. During the Tang dynasty, Chinese poetry, art, and trade flourished.

In the Five Dynasties period (907–960), China again was divided between north and south. Part of northern China was ruled by ethnic minorities, and the south was divided into a number of smaller states. The country was united once again

A Tang dynasty carving depicting Prince Siddhartha Gautama in meditation

under the Song (960–1279). The Song emperors were great patrons of the arts. Chinese painting, calligraphy, and poetry, known as the Three Perfections, became the hallmark of the Chinese elite.

The threat of nomadic peoples in the north had long been a concern to the settled farmers of China. One group, the Mongols, under the leadership of Kublai Khan, defeated the Song and established the Yuan dynasty in 1279. During the Yuan, which lasted until 1368, international trade along the Silk Routes thrived. In the West, China's reputation for luxury goods inspired the Venetian traveler Marco Polo to visit China. The Yuan established the Chinese capital at Beijing.

A Western representation of Marco Polo being welcomed at the court of Kublai Khan

The Mongols were driven from power by the Ming (1368–1644). The new native Chinese dynasty expanded the capital at Beijing. The city was supplied with grain by improving the Grand Canal to ship grain from the south. During the Ming dynasty, China's luxury goods flourished, and maritime trade reached the east coast of Africa.

Founded in 1644 by Manchu people from the north of China, the Qing dynasty lasted until 1911. It was China's last dynasty.

The middle part of the Qing dynasty was marked by able rulers and the expansion of the Chinese empire to its greatest limits, including Mongolia and Tibet. The people enjoyed low taxation. Massive irrigation projects ordered by the Qing emperors benefited the farmers.

The great skill of Qing leaders resulted in a concentration of power in the emperor. This proved too great a responsibility for Qing rulers by the end of the dynasty.

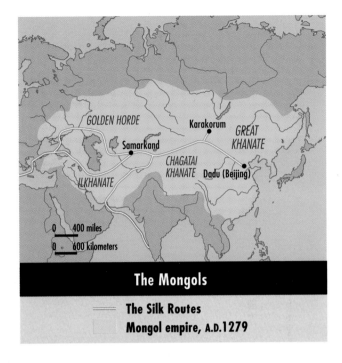

The Mongols

— **The Silk Routes**
Mongol empire, A.D.1279

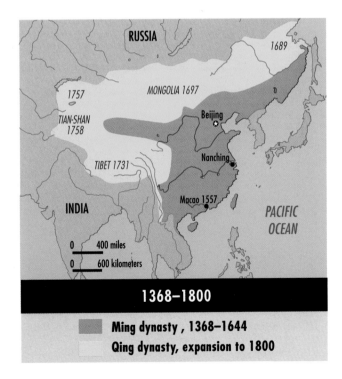

1368–1800

 Ming dynasty , 1368–1644
 Qing dynasty, expansion to 1800

Late Qing emperors modeled their rule on that of the previous Chinese dynasty, the Ming dynasty. Inward-looking isolationism and conservative thinking came to characterize the late Qing. At the same time, technological and scientific revolutions were taking place in the West. As a result, when the foreign powers reached China's shores, the Qing emperors were unable to respond as military equals.

Foreign Influence

Like the Manchus before them, Europeans, Japanese, and Americans could not be held back by the Great Wall. They arrived by sea at China's coast demanding to become trading partners. The foreigners wanted China's silk, tea, and spices.

A Western depiction of an attack on Chinese ships during the First Opium War

Seeking goods that the Chinese would buy from them in exchange, some traders brought opium to Chinese shores.

In 1800, the Qing emperor banned opium trade in China. Foreign powers ignored the order and continued to make money selling opium. Enraged, the Chinese seized 20,000 chests of British opium brought to Guangzhou (Canton) from India in 1839. The British responded by attacking and defeating Chinese forces. This was the first of four Opium Wars.

Each war ended with a humiliating treaty for China and the establishment of seaports to receive foreign goods. Soon, a string of Treaty Ports stretched across the map of China.

These ports were a second home to foreign political delegations and traders. They built Western-style homes, churches, and schools in foreign compounds where Chinese were forbidden to live. The Chinese became second-class citizens in their own country.

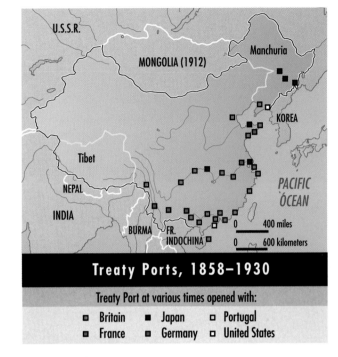

Treaty Ports, 1858–1930

Treaty Port at various times opened with:

- Britain
- France
- Japan
- Germany
- Portugal
- United States

The Chinese could no longer tolerate these conditions. In Guangzhou, a man claiming to be the younger brother of Jesus Christ arose to preach Christianity and reform. The movement was called Heavenly Kingdom of the Great Peace, or Taiping. In many ways, this was a forerunner of the Communist movement in the following century. The Chinese were attracted by policies of public ownership of farms, fairer taxes, and the banning of slavery.

The Qing government saw Taiping calls for reform as a threat to the throne. Foreign powers preferred to deal with the weakened Qing government. In 1860, the two formed an alliance and defeated the Taipings.

Now the foreigners carved up China into "spheres of influence." By 1898, Russia, Germany, Britain, Japan, and France all claimed a piece of China. But the United States proposed an "open door" policy, leaving China open to trade with any foreign power. China was at the mercy of foreigners. The Chinese people demanded a change.

The Boxers

A new set of rebels now emerged. The "Righteous and Harmonious Fists" developed a form of boxing that prepared the body and mind for combat. Their slogan was "Overthrow the Qing and destroy the foreigners."

But the Qing throne saw the Boxers as a useful way to rid the country of foreigners. After first fighting them, the Qing united with the Boxers in an antiforeigner alliance. The massacre of Chinese Christians, missionaries, and other foreigners began. In 1900, the foreigners' compound in Beijing was attacked.

Western powers responded with a new defeat of the Chinese. China became a nation in name only. Organizations calling for the end of the Qing dynasty were being set up across the country.

The Chinese Republic

The Alliance for Chinese Revolution was headed by Sun Yat-sen, who wished to found a China on the ideas of democracy. Sun was proclaimed president of the Chinese Republic in 1912.

Although there was a national government in Beijing, the capital city, the real power was in the hands of warlords. These were regional strongmen who ruled and kept their power through violence.

Sun Yat-sen

Sun Yat-sen, the father of the first Republic of China, was a medical doctor who was educated in Japan. Sun's efforts to establish a Chinese republic enjoyed the support of educated Chinese as well as overseas Chinese who helped finance his efforts.

Sun's republic was based on the Three Principles of the People: love the fatherland, democracy, and welfare of the Chinese people.

The warlords were constantly involved in struggles for expansion and in a series of broken political agreements. These included treaties and alliances with one another as well as with European powers.

Many of China's major cities were treaty ports with foreign enclaves. Here, taxes on Chinese export goods were kept artificially low by foreign powers. Customs and salt revenues collected within China were used as payment for China's foreign obligations instead of for the welfare of the Chinese people.

The Imperial Examination System was no longer in place to reward learning. Since the Han dynasty, China had been governed by men who did well in these exams. They had earned their high positions in the emperor's court. This meant that the meritocracy—rule by those who had earned their positions by talent and intelligence—no longer existed in China.

With the examination system abolished, wealthy Chinese people had no hope of using their talents in government service. Some became landlords, pure and simple. Others left China to study in Europe, the United States, and Japan. Returning students brought a flood of new ideas into China.

On May 4, 1919, thousands of students in Beijing took to the streets of the city in a great political protest. These students were protesting new interference in China's affairs by foreign powers.

In World War I (1914-1918), China had entered on the Allied side, with Britain, France, and the United States. China sent workers to France, where manpower was critically short. Yet the Treaty of Versailles, drawn up by the Allied forces after Germany's defeat, ignored China. The defeated Germans were told to transfer their Chinese treaty ports to the Japanese instead of returning them to China.

The Chinese students were outraged. Their protest was marked by violence and arrests. More protests followed.

In the end, China never signed the Treaty of Versailles. The government in Beijing backed down and the arrested students were released. Public support for the students continued to grow and became known as the May Fourth Movement.

The strong Chinese nationalism of the May Fourth Movement affected China's future political struggles. Today, the term May Fourth Movement is used to refer to the turbulent political period from 1915 to the 1920s. During this period, many elements of China's traditional culture were rejected and new ideas were sought. Chief among these was the permanent rejection of Confucianism and increased social action, especially in the organizing of labor unions. This became crucial in the struggle that led to the founding of the People's Republic of China in 1949.

But the new Chinese Republic existed in name only. Sun did not have the power to rule. The power was in the hands of those who controlled the military. Struggles between military factions led by warlords made the nation unstable. Then new threats to China came from Japan.

New Political Parties

China's intellectuals sought a new solution in the theories of Marx and Lenin. At Beijing University, a librarian helped found the Chinese Communist Party. He was joined by a young man named Mao Zedong. In the city of Tianjin, a Communist study group was started by a man named Zhou Enlai.

Mao Zedong

Mao Zedong came from a peasant family and saw the unequal distribution of wealth and resources in China. The hardworking peasants, mainly small farmers, lived in poverty, while landlords owned large areas of land and had considerable wealth. Mao Zedong's dream for China was a Communist government that was said to be based on the idea that everyone works together for the good of all the people, and all people are equal.

The Changing Role of Women

In traditional China, the role of women was defined by the Three Confucian Obediences: to the father before marriage, to the husband after marriage, and to sons in widowhood. During this time, the lives of most Chinese women were spent within the family.

During the first half of the 1900s, Chinese intellectuals began to question and reject many of the values of Confucian society. Instead, they favored individual freedom and equality of men and women. During these decades, Chinese women made limited progress in education, employment outside the home, and political organization.

Increasingly, as China's political struggles intensified, many Chinese came to believe that the low status of women and the narrow scope of their activities were among the basic causes of national weakness and poverty. The emancipation of women was seen as a necessary part of the liberation of China.

During the May Fourth Movement, many women took part in political demonstrations. In the years of struggle between the Communists and the Nationalists, women earned recognition working with fellow revolutionaries, including participation in the Communists' Long March in 1934 and 1935.

Under Mao's Communist government, established with the founding of the People's Republic of China in 1949, Chinese women assumed, in theory, an equal status with men. Mao proclaimed: "Women hold up half the sky." He was referring to women's involvement in every aspect of the new nation.

To build a new China, women were asked to replace their traditional dedication to the family with self-sacrifice for the nation. Now women had the chance to contribute to the family, Chinese society, and the nation.

Increasingly, Chinese women have come to see their role divided between traditional reproduction for family and the production of goods for the nation. To show their increased concern with women's needs and rights, the Chinese government hosted the United Nations Fourth World Conference on Women in 1995.

At the same time, the Kuomintang, or Nationalist Party, which emerged after the abdication of the Qing, began to train its National Revolutionary Army. This army was led by Chiang Kai-shek. His plans for China were based on traditional rule by a small group. Together, Chiang and Mao, each with a different view for China's future, began efforts to unite and modernize China while getting rid of foreign aggressors.

Chiang was appointed commander-in-chief of the National Revolutionary Army by both the Kuomintang and the Communists. Troops began an effort to take power away from warlords in northern China and to fight the Japanese who had invaded China.

Civil War

It soon became clear that the Kuomintang and the Communists could not work together. A civil war began for control of the country. Chiang summed up his feelings about his two enemies in this way:

The Japanese are a disease of the skin.

The Communists are a disease of the heart.

Poorly equipped and small in number, the Communists adopted the strategy of guerrilla warfare. Their strategy was summed up in a slogan:

The enemy advances, we retreat;

The enemy camps, we harass;

The enemy tires, we attack;

The enemy retreats, we pursue.

Generalissimo Chiang Kai-shek after having been presented with the U.S. Legion of Merit Medal

Survivors of the Long March

The Long March

When Chiang's troops hemmed in 90,000 Communist troops in southern China, the Communists began a retreat to the north. They marched across some of the world's harshest terrain. This legendary Communist retreat, called the Long March, took an entire year and covered some 6,000 miles (9,700 km).

As the Communists trekked through China's remote and poor areas, they took lands away from wealthy landlords and gave them to poor peasants. Many of these peasants joined the Communist troops. They were issued guns that had been captured from the Nationalists. But sickness, fatigue, and exposure took a terrible toll on the Communist troops. Only 20,000 men and women completed the Long March. Mao Zedong and Zhou Enlai were among the survivors.

The Long March proved, however, that China's peasants would fight for Communism if they were given guns and hope. The power base for the Communists was not the educated class living in China's cities. It was the farming peasants. Mao and Zhou had learned an important lesson.

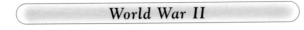

World War II

When the Japanese bombed Pearl Harbor in 1941, the United States hoped to use China as a base for attacking Japanese troops and shipping routes. Chiang hoped the Americans would then arm his troops so that he could defeat the Chinese Communists.

Chiang was afraid that once the Nazis were defeated in Europe, the Russians would invade China and set up a Communist government. However, the Soviet leader, Josef Stalin, felt that once the war with Japan was over, the Nationalists' well-equipped army of more than 2.5 million troops would quickly defeat the Communist forces. So Stalin urged the Chinese Communists to form a new alliance with the Nationalists.

But Mao and his Communist troops had fought too long and too hard. They knew they had the backing of China's farming peasants, the vast majority of China's population. When Japan surrendered in 1945, Communist armies and Nationalist armies began their final battle for control of China.

Shanghai suburbs, where in 1949 each family was required to send someone to dig trenches for three days.

Residents of Shanghai celebrate the founding of the People's Republic of China. Young students carry a portrait of Mao Zedong.

Tiananmen Square

Tiananmen Square in Beijing is the symbolic center of today's China. The name of the square means "Gate of Heavenly Peace" or "Gate of Heavenly Stability." This name comes from the gate that guarded the southern approach to Beijing's Forbidden City. This was the home of the emperors of the Ming and Qing dynasties and the administrative headquarters of the imperial government.

Communist Victory

Nationalist troops occupied China's major cities. The Communist troops had their power bases in the countryside. Now, Nationalist troops found themselves outnumbered and surrounded by Communist forces. Thousands of Chiang's troops switched sides and joined the Communists in their fight for a new China.

The city of Nanjing, the Nationalist capital, fell to the Communists in April 1949 when Communist troops crossed the Yangze River in a fleet of small fishing boats. The Nationalists fled to Guangzhou and then to Chongqing as the Communists took all the major cities south of the Yangze.

Finally, Chiang fled to the island of Taiwan. More than 2 million Nationalists followed him. He planned to return to mainland China and reclaim it in the near future.

On October 1, 1949, Mao Zedong, now chairman of the Chinese Communist Party, proclaimed the foundation of the People's Republic of China. Speaking in Tiananmen Square, Mao proclaimed a new China based upon the fair distribution of land and goods and equality of all China's people.

Taiwan

Taiwan, the island to which Chiang Kai-shek and Nationalist Chinese troops fled in 1949 is currently governed by Chinese as the Republic of China. Taiwan Chinese have refused to submit to the Communist government of the People's Republic of China. They enjoy a democratic form of government with free elections.

The people of Taiwan consider themselves to be the upholders of traditional Chinese values. They are highly educated and have built up a booming economy.

The Cultural Revolution

Tiananmen Square has provided a stage for some of the most important events in the history of the People's Republic of China. By 1966, Mao's economic policies had led to famine in China. In order to regain his political power, Mao designed an attack on his political opponents in the Chinese Communist Party and government. This became the Cultural Revolution.

From 1966 to 1976, during the Cultural Revolution, tens of thousands of young Chinese became Red Guards. Red Guards rallied to Tiananmen Square to pledge their loyalty to Mao. They carried copies of *Quotations from Chairman Mao Zedong,* a collection of Mao's sayings and political thought known as the *Little Red Book.*

A propaganda poster from the Cultural Revolution proclaims, "Long live the glorious Chinese Communist Party".

The Red Guards attacked Chinese Communist Party bureaucracy, claiming to root out the evils of the old society and the elite in Chinese society. Included in the attacks were intellectuals, teachers, scientists, and politicians, including Zhou Enlai. They were sent to the countryside for "reeducation" through hard labor. Monuments and temples were destroyed, and religious worship was forbidden. There was chaos throughout the country.

In 1972, U.S. president Richard Nixon and Mao toasted each other in the

WEI DA DE ZHONG GUO GONG CHAN DANG WAN SUI

Red Guards in 1966, marching with flags and beating drums while carrying a portrait of their idol, Mao Zedong

Mao Zedong with President Richard Nixon

Great Hall of the People in Tiananmen Square. Their meeting marked the opening of the "Bamboo Curtain"—the renewal of diplomatic relations between China and the United States.

After Mao's death in 1976, his widow and three bureaucrats emerged as the governing power in China. Quickly denounced as the Gang of Four, they were toppled from power and imprisoned.

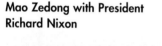

Leadership for the Future

Deng Xiaoping assumed the guidance of China's government with policies of moderation and modernization. A Communist revolutionary, Deng had played a major role in the Civil War that led to the founding of the People's Republic of China.

Deng's death in 1997 brought an end to the era of government by people who had fought alongside Mao in the Communist Revolution. Leadership was assumed by President Jiang Zemin, an engineer by training and the former mayor of Shanghai.

In 1989, Tiananmen Square again became the focal point of Chinese politics. Students were protesting corruption of the *ganbu,* or Communist officials, as well as calling for democracy and greater equality among Chinese people. After weeks of demonstrations, thousands of armed soldiers from the People's Liberation Army opened fire on the demonstrators. The incident, known as the Tiananmen Square Massacre or the June 4th Massacre, set off international protest.

In 1997, Tiananmen Square was the site of a massive celebration. Hong Kong, a port leased to the British for one hundred years after defeat of the Qing army during the Opium Wars, was returned to China. As the Union Jack of Great Britain was lowered, the red flag of China was raised above the former colony, and thousands gathered in Tiananmen Square to celebrate.

In 1998, President Bill Clinton was the guest of President Jiang Zemin as he toured the People's Republic of China. In the Great Hall of the People, the leaders of two of the world's most powerful nations exchanged ideas in a lively debate broadcast live on Chinese TV.

A prodemocracy demonstration in Hong Kong before its transfer to China

Governing One Billion People

In a population more than 1 billion strong, the government depends upon the willing help and contribution of every man, woman, and child. The government in the People's Republic of China is a continuity of both China's past traditions and the twentieth-century thinking of Mao Zedong.

I N IMPERIAL CHINA, CONFUCIANISM WAS THE PHILOSOPHY
that regulated society. Confucius developed a unique moral
outlook based on the belief that man is basically good. In
Confucianism, the role of government is to establish and
maintain an orderly network of human relations and behavior.
The political philosophy of Mao Zedong is similar to that of
Confucius in its emphasis on human relations as the building
blocks of a stable and just society.

Opposite: **A crowd of schoolchildren from the Hunan Province**

The PRC Constitution

The Constitution of the People's Republic of China specifies
that the country's central governing body is to be made up of

Confucius

Confucius (551–479 B.C.) lived
during the Warring States period
of the Zhou dynasty, a time of
constant warfare. He traveled to
each state in turn, seeking to convince each ruler that a more
perfect society could be formed
when rulers and subjects, nobles
and peasants, and all family
members devoted themselves to
their responsibilities to others.

five sections formed by the National People's Congress (NPC). The NPC has elected officials who make up the Standing Committee of the National People's Congress.

The five sections responsible to the NPC and its Standing Committee are the Presidency, the State Council, the Central Military Commission, the Supreme People's Court, and the Supreme People's Procuratorate.

The NPC is the highest government power of the People's Republic of China. Its main functions and powers include making laws, delegating authority, making policy, and supervising other government departments.

Under the current Constitution, the NPC holds a session in the first quarter of each year, convened by its Standing Committee. Standing Committee members of the NPC are elected to office for a term of five years.

NATIONAL PEOPLE'S CONGRESS

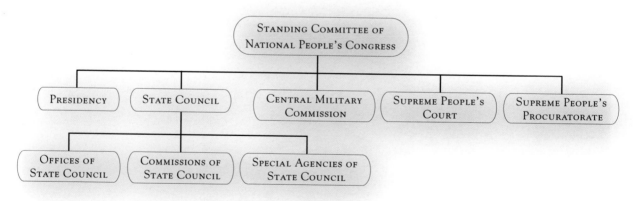

The first session of the ninth National People's Congress, held in the Great Hall of the People, Tiananmen Square

The Presidency

The president of the People's Republic of China is the head of state. He is also the supreme representative of China both nationally and internationally. As in other countries, the president holds supreme diplomatic and ceremonial rights.

However, China has a system of collective leadership. The president is subordinate to the NPC and directly receives instructions from this group.

Deng Xiaoping (left) and President Jiang Zemin (right) in Shanghai

The State Council

The State Council of the PRC is the highest executive section of power and administration. The State Council is composed of a premier, vice premiers, state councillors, ministers in charge of ministries and commissions, the auditor general, and the secretary general.

The State Council carries out the principles and policies of the Communist Party of China as well as the regulations and laws adopted by the NPC. It also deals with China's internal politics, diplomacy, national defense, finance, economy, culture, and education.

The Central Military Commission

The People's Liberation Army (PLA) has three branches: the army, the air force, and the navy. The role of China's military is to safeguard national sovereignty, territorial integrity, and world peace.

The chairman of the Central Military Commission is elected by the NPC. Under the leadership of the Central Military Commission, the Chinese army has been reformed, streamlined, and reorganized in recent years. It currently includes 3 million troops.

During the Chinese Communist Revolution, PLA members helped to recruit civilians to the Communist cause. For this reason, the PLA has played a major role in China's government since the establishment of the People's Republic of China in 1949.

Both men and women serve in the PLA. Admission to the military is voluntary. The minimum age for service is

eighteen. It is considered a great honor to be chosen to serve.
Unlike the highly stratified ranks of Western armies, there is
equality within the Chinese ranks.

Members of the PLA are said to embody ideal Communist
virtues: honesty and loyalty, bravery, selflessness, and initiative. The events of June 4, 1989, at Tiananmen Square were a
devastating blow to the image and prestige of the People's
Liberation Army.

On August 1 each year, the country honors the men
and women in the military. Song-and-dance ensembles of military units entertain millions of Chinese on state television.
They perform patriotic songs, folk songs, dances, and popular
music. Life in the PLA is often the subject of popular daytime
television dramas.

The Hong Kong handover ceremonies on July 1, 1997

In 1997, the PLA had a major presence in the ceremonies marking the return of Hong Kong to China. While Western journalists reported this event as a show of force, others claim it demonstrated China preferred to wait until the return could be achieved via diplomatic means rather than military force.

The Supreme People's Court

The Supreme People's Court is the highest court of law in China. It is responsible to the NPC and its Standing Committee. According to the Constitution, the Supreme People's Court has three responsibilities: trying cases that have the greatest influence in China and hearing appeals against the legal decisions of other courts; supervising the work of local courts and special courts at every level and overruling wrong judgments they might have made; and giving judicial explanations of specific utilization of laws that must be carried out nationwide.

The Supreme People's Procuratorate

The people's procuratorates are state departments for legal supervision. The Supreme People's Procuratorate is the nation's highest procuratorial department. It is mainly responsible for supervising regional and special procuratorates. The Supreme People's Procuratorate reports to the NPC and its Standing Committee.

The Communist Party of China (CPC) was founded on July 1, 1921, in Shanghai. The CPC is the ruling party of China and the sole representative of the interests of the Chinese nation.

The CPC acts as the vanguard of the people. In leading the rest of Chinese society to Communist goals, the CPC sets policy that is then set in motion by the state.

Currently, the CPC has more than 55 million members. *Renmin Ribao (People's Daily)* is the official newspaper of the CPC Central Committee.

According to Chinese Communists, all human behavior is based upon a sense of morality. This morality arose from previous class struggles between the few wealthy landowners and the masses of Chinese peasants who worked the land.

In 1949, the rulers of the newly formed People's Republic of China set out to destroy every existing social institution in China and replace them all with Communism. They began a series of campaigns, movements, propaganda, and executions. The purpose was to wipe out any source of power, information, and authority that was not under the control of the Chinese Communist Party.

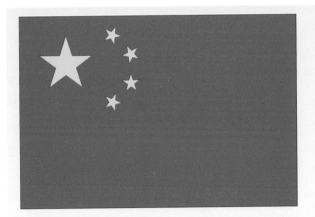

The national flag of the People's Republic of China has a bold red background and five yellow stars in the upper-left corner. The red background symbolizes revolution. One large five-pointed star is next to four smaller five-pointed stars. The large star represents the Communist Party of China, and the four smaller stars represent the Chinese people. The position of the stars represents the unity of the Chinese people under the leadership of the Communist Party.

From these efforts, a new two-class society emerged in China. Communist society is now composed of *ganbu*, those who provide political leadership, and the peasant masses they govern. Communist philosophy holds that the interest of the two classes is the same. The two classes are supposed to work together for the common good of China.

Justice

China's judicial system works to protect the basic rights, freedoms, and interests of all citizens in accordance with the law. It is set up to protect public property, maintain social order, guarantee smooth progress of the modernization drive, and punish criminals according to the law.

The court system in China breaks cases into five categories: criminal law, civil law, economic law, maritime law, and administrative law. Civil law accounts for the greatest number of cases. It includes marital proceedings such as divorce. Administrative law includes cases of intellectual property rights.

People guilty of petty crimes, such as theft, might be sentenced to publicly confess their crime in front of their fellow workers. This public humiliation is intended to help criminals repent their crime and prevent a repetition of the behavior. China also has a prison system where criminals are sent to be reformed. Some of these prisons require inmates to work in farming or manufacturing.

A criminal may be sentenced to death for a serious crime. Chinese consider such crimes to include not only violent acts, as in the West, but also bribery, corruption, and misappropriation of funds. On occasion, these death sentences are carried out in public or even broadcast on TV. The condemned criminals are executed by firing squad.

An example of this was the execution of a group of criminals who had manufactured a worthless medicine that looked like a real medicine. They sold this medicine for high prices. Much suffering was experienced by those in need of the medicine, and some people died. This sort of economic crime could not be tolerated in China. The criminals received a death sentence by firing squad.

Beijing: Did You Know This?

Beijing straddles the traditional divide between Inner and Outer China. The name *Beijing* means "northern capital." The city was made the capital by the Mongols during the Yuan dynasty.

Population: 11,299,000 (1995 est.)

Altitude: 600 feet (183 m)

Average Daily Temperature:

24°F (−4.4°C) in January

79°F (26°C) in July

Average Annual Rainfall: 25 inches (64 cm)

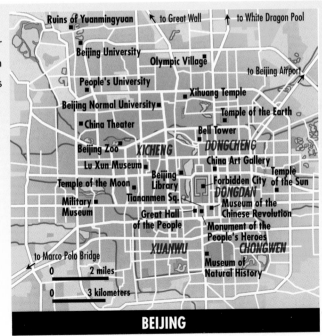

CHAPTER SIX

Feeding the Masses

Most Chinese in today's economy, as in the past, work on the land. China must produce enough food to feed more than 1 billion people. This is four times the population of the United States, but China has less farmland than the United States has.

F EEDING ITS PEOPLE WITHOUT RELY-
ing on other countries has been a top
priority of the government since the
founding of the People's Republic of
China in 1949. Only 15 percent of
Chinese territory is farmland, and
much of it is vulnerable to flood and
drought. The stability of the country
rests on the government's ability to
safeguard the livelihood of its people.
How can it feed a billion people?

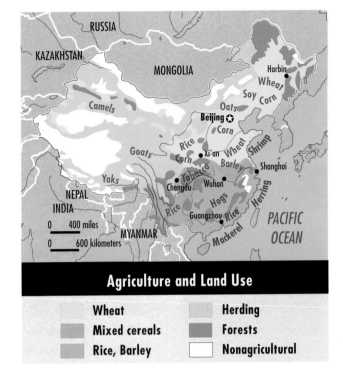

Agriculture and Land Use

Wheat	Herding
Mixed cereals	Forests
Rice, Barley	Nonagricultural

The Chinese government believes the answer lies in a
two-fold plan: modernization and population control. A series
of hydroengineering projects must be completed to control
floods. Irrigation channels must be built to expand farmland.
And the nation's transportation network must be
upgraded to carry agricultural and
manufactured products to wherever
they are needed.

The government also has an
aggressive campaign of birth control
to limit population growth. Each Han
Chinese family may have only one
child. Minority groups are allowed to
have more.

Opposite: **Rice farmers
working in a field in
Sichuan Province**

**A billboard in Shanghai
promoting the "One Child
Only" campaign**

Feeding the Masses **75**

Imperial Economy

Chinese farmers were the foundation of Imperial China. Farmers paid their taxes by giving a certain amount of grain to the government. This grain was distributed to the army that defended China's frontiers and to pay the scholar-officials who ran the empire. The emperor offered prayers to heaven asking for a bountiful harvest for each coming year. Surplus grain was stored in government granaries to be distributed to the needy in times of famine.

Rice and Millet

In northern China, farmers cultivate millet and wheat on the plains and on the fertile loess plateau. To raise crops on the loess plateau, farmers developed terrace farming. The hillsides were cut into a series of steplike terraces. The terraces wind around the hillsides in long, narrow fields to maximize the fertile areas.

In south China, rice is grown in well-irrigated river valleys. Rice paddies are dug into the earth and surrounded by low dikes to control irrigation. Traditionally, men plow and irrigate the rice paddies and women weed the crop.

In Imperial China, the production and distribution of many items essential for daily living, such as salt and iron, were handled only by the state. In addition, large state factories manufactured goods such as porcelain and lacquerware.

For these reasons, large-scale industries were established earlier in China than in the West. Such state industries served as models for private enterprises and led to early industrialization.

During the years of war preceding the founding of the People's Republic of China, the country was torn by the Japanese invasion and the civil war between the Nationalists and the Communists. Many irrigation systems broke down, and livestock and animal populations were severely reduced. Agricultural output also dropped drastically. Famine and disease were rampant.

Mao, who called himself the "Great Peasant Leader," carried out a series of reforms in rural areas. The scarcity of farmland, overpopulation, and peasant indebtedness to landlords all had to be overcome. Mao's most important program was Land Reform.

Before Land Reform, tenant farmers were controlled by landlords, much like sharecroppers in the American south. Throughout the 1950s, land was taken from the landlords, and

Farmers transplanting rice seedlings in Yunnan Province

commmunes, or collective farms, were established throughout the country. Communes were large farms run by the government. Land was nationalized.

Manufacturing

While efficiency in agriculture was crucial to China's survival, manufacturing was not a primary concern. The economic policies of Communist China stressed willpower and effort more than efficiency.

In 1958, an economic movement called the Great Leap Forward began. Mao believed that China's industrialization could be dramatically accelerated by an all-out effort. A massive propaganda campaign involving every man, woman, and child in the People's Republic of China began.

To build heavy industry, China imported machinery from the Soviet Union. To pay for these imports, Chinese exported large quantities of agricultural products and raw materials.

The government thought centralization could lead to a more efficient use of land and other resources. Some communes consisted of tens of thousands of farmers. Many of these farmers were assigned to work on the development of local industrial projects, such as small steel furnaces, fertilizer plants, dams, and other irrigation projects.

The central planners had overestimated the regional and national output, and many local officials exaggerated the result of local efforts. As a result, the central planners made unrealistic projections and plans, which, in turn, put pressure on local officials to meet unrealistic production targets. Mismanagement and resource dislocation were the inevitable outcome. To make the situation worse, flood and drought ruined the harvests of 1959 and 1960.

When China refused to let the Soviet Union control its natural resources, infrastructure, and military, the Soviet Union withdrew its technical specialists. This left China with many unfinished industrial projects.

China suffered a severe famine from 1959 to 1961. When the Soviet government withdrew its technical specialists, it also revoked its agreement to supply surplus wheat to China to avoid food shortages. It is estimated that 30 million people died of starvation during these years. It was a human tragedy on a massive scale.

Deng Xiaoping was more pragmatic in managing China's economy than Mao. He wanted to stimulate economic growth

What China Grows, Makes, and Mines

Agriculture

Rice	178,251,000 metric tons
Corn (maize)	103,550,000 metric tons
Wheat	101,205,000 metric tons

Manufacturing

Cement	450,000,000 metric tons
Rolled steel	80,000,000 metric tons
Chemical fertilizer	24,500,000 metric tons

Mining

Iron ore	234,000,000 metric tons
Salt	32,000,000 metric tons
Gypsum	11,000,000 metric tons

Pollution

Pollution in China is severe. In its race to industrialize, the Chinese government neglected to safeguard its water, air, and land against industrial pollution. The government is now facing the task of a massive environmental cleanup while trying to maintain China's recent impressive economic growth.

Time named Deng Xiaoping Man of the Year for 1978 and 1985 (below). He is one of only nine men to achieve this distinction more than once.

Deng Xiaoping

with practical incentives first and political motivations a distant second. To eliminate famine and become self-sufficient in food supply now became the primary concern of the government.

Large communes were abolished under Deng. Although land remained nationalized, land-use decisions were left to the farmers. Free markets and prime plots of land on lease were established. Agricultural output improved significantly.

To Mao, these new policies spelled a return to China's capitalist past. He labeled economic reformers "capitalist roaders." During the Cultural Revolution, Mao had forced Deng out of power and sent him to a labor camp for "reeducation." Later, Deng was recalled by Mao. After Mao's death in 1976 and the downfall of the Gang of Four, Deng Xiaoping returned to power and carried out his economic reforms.

Today, China's economic system is in transition. It is moving toward a market economy. Communes were largely eliminated by 1984. Production decisions are now in the hands of the farmers. State enterprises are moving in the direction of privatization and collective ownership. Foreign technology and foreign investment are welcomed in China today.

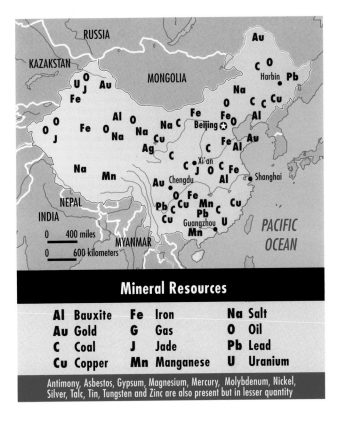

Mineral Resources

Al	Bauxite	**Fe**	Iron	**Na**	Salt
Au	Gold	**G**	Gas	**O**	Oil
C	Coal	**J**	Jade	**Pb**	Lead
Cu	Copper	**Mn**	Manganese	**U**	Uranium

Antimony, Asbestos, Gypsum, Magnesium, Mercury, Molybdenum, Nickel, Silver, Talc, Tin, Tungsten and Zinc are also present but in lesser quantity

The growth of light industry and heavy industry are almost equal. Construction industry is developing steadily. Geological prospecting has uncovered natural resources including petroleum, natural gas, coal, iron ore, sulfuric ore, and gold.

Transport and Telecommunications

There has been significant improvement in transportation too. Railway, highway, and airway freight have all increased, as has cargo handled at major ports and inland waterways. Computer network services, fax machines, and mobile telephones have dramatically improved China's communication systems.

China's government has established many new economic zones to encourage capital formation and attract foreign investment. Chinese who live in Taiwan, Hong Kong, Singapore, and North America are important sources of capital investment in China. These ethnic Chinese seek to gain both economic profit and personal satisfaction by helping to rebuild mainland China.

A Volkswagen assembly line in Shanghai

During President Clinton's 1998 state visit to China, he stressed the importance of economic cooperation between the two countries. China's trading status with the United States as a most favored nation was renewed.

The Chinese Stock Market

In no other region of the world are investors emerging as rapidly as they are in the Asian-Pacific region. The Chinese government, on an aggressive economic campaign to improve China's infrastructure, has issued bonds now owned by hundreds of millions of people. Those who dabble in China's stock markets number in the tens of millions.

Currency

Renminbi (people's money) is issued by the People's Bank of China. The basic unit of Chinese currency is the *yuan*. The yuan is further divided into ten *jiao*. Each jiao is made up by ten *fen*. Yuan are issued in 1, 2, 5, 10, 50, and 100 paper note denominations; jiao, in 1, 2, and 5 denominations. Coins are issued in 1, 2, and 5 fen. In 1999, 8.28 yuan equaled U.S.$1.

The national emblem of the People's Republic of China can be seen on China's currency. It is circular in shape, with ears of grain and a cogwheel as the border. An image of Tiananmen is in the center, with five stars located above. Tiananmen represents the spirit of the Chinese people in their fight against imperialism and feudalism; the ears of grain and the cogwheel symbolize the working class and the peasants; and the stars again signify the unity of the Chinese people under the leadership of the Communist Party.

The Chinese government has set limits on the percentage of a business that can be owned by foreign investors. It has done this by selling two kinds of shares—Class A shares for Chinese citizens only, and Class B shares for everyone else. This policy is intended to encourage foreign investment while retaining some control over the Chinese economy. Investors can track the movements of the Shanghai and Shenzhen stock markets by reading *The Asian Wall Street Journal.*

Pedestrians in front of a McDonald's restaurant in Beijing

Labor System

Before 1978, workers living in cities were assigned to jobs. In the public sector, wages were fixed. In the collective sector, such as collective farms or factories, the workers' wages were determined by a system that failed to reward individual productivity. The Chinese called this system the "iron rice bowl." This policy practically turned employment in the government sector into a welfare system.

In 1978, premium and piecework systems and bonus systems, which had been abolished in the Cultural Revolution, were restored.

In 1986, the State Council announced new regulations, under which workers were to be given contracts under terms that allowed for their dismissal. The reform of the labor system and the creation of a labor market have stimulated the economy.

The People's Bank of China

The People's Bank of China is the country's central bank. Like other central banks, it distributes currency, sets monetary policy, and monitors the financial workings of the country.

Hong Kong

In the nineteenth century, Great Britain imposed three unequal treaties on China, thus occupying and leasing Hong Kong by force. On July 1, 1997, Hong Kong rejoined China.

The system of "one country, two systems" was proposed by Deng Xiaoping. It stated that Hong Kong would enjoy a high degree of self-rule. The economic system of Hong Kong would remain unchanged for many years. Hong Kong was also free to maintain and develop relations with other countries.

Expatriates from around the world enjoy the lifestyle of Hong Kong and the availability of foreign products. English-language newspapers and TV and radio broadcasts continue to be produced.

A busy street scene in the Central District of Hong Kong

Recently, however, a series of economic disasters have affected Hong Kong. The first of these was the outbreak of a poultry flu that is still a mystery to international researchers. The latest economic disaster was the opening of the Hong Kong International Airport. This multibillion-dollar project has been dogged by mismanagement and has been a major headache for importers.

A Hong Kong cityscape

More seriously, the market value of real estate and the stock market have suffered dramatic declines. The collapse of the unstable economies of several Asian countries has had a serious impact on the Hong Kong economy. It remains to be seen whether China will be able to maintain its economic growth and political stability.

China's Systems of Weights and Measures

The People's Republic of China uses the metric system for international trade. Within the nation, the Chinese weigh and measure quantities according to their own traditional system. The chart below shows some Chinese weights and measures.

1 chi	1.09 feet	(0.33 m)
1 li	0.31 mile	(0.50 km)
1 mu	0.16 acre	(0.06 ha)
1 jin	1.10 pounds	(0.50 kg)
1 shen	0.22 gallon	(1.00 l)

People of the People's Republic

The People's Republic of China is the most populous nation in the world. One in every five people in the world is Chinese. China's population is four times that of the United States, yet the Chinese have only a little more land area.

T HE VAST MAJORITY OF CHINESE ARE
considered to be Han Chinese, descendants of China's first great dynasty, the
Han. All Han Chinese speak the same
language, Mandarin Chinese, and share
the same cultural traditions.

The government of the People's
Republic of China also recognizes 55
minorities. These minority people
make up about 8 percent of China's
population, and they are spread out
over about half of China's territory.
Many minorities live in Outer China,
especially the borderlands such as Tibet,
Mongolia, Xinjiang, and Xishuangbanna.

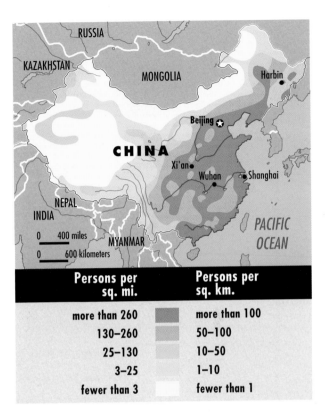

Persons per sq. mi.		Persons per sq. km.
more than 260		more than 100
130–260		50–100
25–130		10–50
3–25		1–10
fewer than 3		fewer than 1

Tibetans

Most of Tibet is an immense plateau at an altitude of 13,123
to 16,404 feet (4,000 to 5,000 m) above sea level. Most
of Tibet's 2 million people live in the valleys in the south of
the country.

Tibetans have their own language, religion, and literature.
Tibetan history begins with invasions of the Tibetan army into
neighboring regions in the seventh century. As the Tibetans
expanded their territory, they controlled Nepal and parts of

Population of Major Cities (1995 est.)

Shanghai	13,584,000
Beijing	11,299,000
Tianjin	9,415,000
Shenyang	5,116,000
Guangzhou	4,492,000

Opposite: **A family from Guizhou Province**

People of the People's Republic **87**

Tibetan women in traditional garb eating barley

Tibetan Buddhist prayer flags and prayer wheels

Yunnan Province as well as the famous Silk Routes, the caravan routes across northern China.

In the ninth century, Tibet was broken up into independent feuding states. As civilian authority decreased, the influence of the Buddhist clergy increased. Tibetan Buddhism adopted many of the customs of *bon*, the traditional religion of the region, including flying prayer flags and turning prayer wheels. *Lamaism*, the monastic side of the religion, involves the meditation of the monks.

After the ninth century, the Buddhist monasteries became increasingly political. The lamas, or monks of the Yellow Hat Sect, were led by a spiritual ruler called the Dalai Lama, which means "Ocean of Wisdom."

Tibetans believe that each Dalai Lama is the reincarnation of the last. When a Dalai Lama dies, the monks search Tibet for the next Dalai Lama. They look for a newborn child who shows some sign of having his predecessor's spirit.

In 1959, the present Dalai Lama fled to India after rebellion broke out between Tibetans and the PLA. More than 80,000 Tibetans fled to India and Nepal, where they still live. Tibet became an autonomous region of China governed from Beijing.

The Golden Dharma Wheel in the Jokhang Temple, Tibet

Mongols

The traditional Mongol homeland lay along the banks of the Onon River, which now forms part of the border between China and Outer Mongolia. Here, in the vast grasslands beyond the Great Wall, the Mongols led a nomadic existence, herding sheep and raising horses.

Today, the Mongols are scattered throughout China's northeastern provinces as well as through Qinghai and Xinjiang. About 1.5 million people live in the Mongolian People's Republic (Outer Mongolia). Inner Mongolia, which stretches across half of northern China, has almost 19 million people, including about 2 million Mongols. The Mongols are now a minority in their own traditional land.

People of the People's Republic   **89**

The major Mongol festival is the annual Nadam Fair held during the summer months on the grasslands. Mongols, living in traditional yurts (tents) made of felt, flock to the festival. Here, they compete in traditional Mongol sports, such as archery, wrestling, and horsemanship.

The Mongols were great horsemen and warriors. In 1206, the various factions of Mongols were united by Genghis Khan. In 1211, they began their conquest of the Chinese. In 1213, they crossed the Great Wall to overcome the Chinese. The Yuan dynasty was founded in 1279 by Ghenghis's grandson, Kublai Khan. Descriptions of the fantastic Yuan capital in Beijing are found in stories told by Marco Polo.

Eventually, the Mongols went on to conquer lands beyond China. Their empire stretched from Burma to Russia—the largest empire in the history of the world.

The eastern expansion of Russia put the Mongols in the middle of border struggles between China and Russia. Northern, or Outer, Mongolia became a Russian protectorate, while Inner Mongolia remained under Chinese rule.

During the 1930s and 1940s, Japan occupied parts of Inner Mongolia. Communist guerrillas fought the Japanese.

Today, the Inner Mongolia Autonomous Region is governed by officials in Beijing. Chinese language is compulsory in school, but Mongols also have their own written language. The Mongols are predominantly Buddhist, with some Muslims among them.

Inner Mongolia is a vast grazing land with an economy based on cattle, sheep, horses, and camels. The region provides China with tanned hides, wool, and dairy products.

Uygurs

Xinjiang covers 16 percent of China's total land area. The region is home to Han Chinese as well as 13 of China's official 55 minority peoples, including Tajiks, Kergezs, Uzbeks, Kazakhs, and Uygurs.

The Uygurs, the largest minority group of the area, are Caucasians. They are larger and heavier than Chinese and their language is Turkish-related.

Uygur women wear long skirts or dresses. Their heads are covered with brightly colored scarves or embroidered caps. The men wear embroidered caps and carry daggers.

The Uygurs are Muslims. Their main food is lamb, barbecued over an open fire. They also raise grapes and melons. The men are famous for their music and the women are known for their graceful dancing.

In the dry climate of Xinjiang, archaeologists have discovered many ancient burial sites. The bodies are well preserved and surrounded by a number of artifacts. Archaeologists have been able to reconstruct ancient Uygur life in Xinjiang by examination of these burial sites.

Uygur women at the market in traditional clothing

Uygur children of Xinjiang Province. Uygurs are the area's largest minority group.

A young Dai girl from the region of Xishuangbanna, Yunnan Province

The Dai

China's most southern province, Yunnan, is home to many minority groups. Located in the deep south of Yunnan near the Laotian border is the region of Xishuangbanna. Here, in the tropical rain forest, live the Dai people. They were driven southward by the Mongol invasion of China in the thirteenth century.

The wooden houses of the Dai people are raised on stilts to keep them off the damp earth of the tropical rain forest. Pigs and chickens are raised below the houses.

The traditional Dai dress is a sarong and a straw hat. The women have upswept hairstyles.

The Dai are Buddhists. Their major holiday is the Water Splashing Festival held in April. The festival is held to wash away the sorrow and demons of the old year and bring happiness for the new.

Unification

Uniting all these different peoples under one flag has been a challenge for the People's Republic of China. Today, there is a strong feeling among most Chinese that non-Han regions are an inseparable part of China.

To strengthen these bonds, the Chinese government has poured vast amounts of material and manpower into the regions inhabited by ethnic peoples. Many of these groups live in harsh conditions that make farming extremely difficult. The government supplies them with grain, fertilizer, and farming equipment.

The government has also built schools to raise the level of education and has attempted to train minority people as government officials. This will further incorporate minority groups into the fabric of Chinese society.

Aging

In 1990, the median age for a citizen of the People's Republic of China was twenty-five. People under the age of fifteen made up about 28 percent of the total population. Citizens over the age of sixty-five accounted for less than 6 percent.

In Old China, the average life expectancy was thirty-four years. Since the founding of the People's Republic of China in 1949, the average life expectancy of the Chinese has doubled. This is due in large part to the rise in the number of health institutions and the availability of medical and health professionals.

The Confucianism of traditional China was centered on filial piety—respect for elders—beginning with respect of children for their parents. This idea included caring for elderly parents and preparing lavish funerals for them.

Since the fall of Confucianism, along with the rise of individual freedom and China's one-child policy, many young Chinese feel that the care of aging parents is no longer their responsibility. Today, many young people expect the state to fill that role. The great respect traditionally given to the elderly seems destined to fade along with other traditions of the Chinese family.

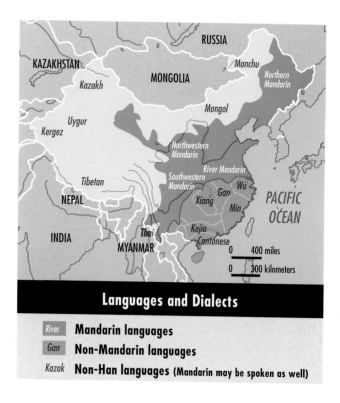

Languages and Dialects

River	**Mandarin languages**
Gan	**Non-Mandarin languages**
Kazak	**Non-Han languages** (Mandarin may be spoken as well)

Language

All citizens of the People's Republic of China are taught Mandarin Chinese in school. Minority people may speak their own language in addition to Mandarin, and Han Chinese may also speak a dialect, such as Cantonese.

In theory, there are almost 60,000 written Chinese characters, but only about 5,000 characters are used in daily life. Most characters from the earliest known examples of Chinese writing are pictographs—pictures of objects, professions, or actions. Most other writing systems eventually developed a phonetic alphabet that represented the sounds of spoken language, just as the Roman alphabet is used to write English. Modern Chinese, however, often still reflects its picture origins.

Writing

Chinese legend tells about the invention of writing more than 5,000 years ago by an official of the mythical Yellow Emperor named Cang Jie. The official, seeing the tracks of birds and animals, devised a system of written characters. At this invention, says the legend, "all the spirits cried out in agony, as the innermost secrets of nature were revealed."

Chinese originally used bamboo strips and silk for writing. During the Han dynasty, an official named Cai Lun invented paper by using bamboo, hemp, and mulberry bark.

Pictographs and Ideographs

Two of the most common types of Chinese characters are pictographs and ideographs. Pictographs are simple drawings of objects. For example, the pictograph for "tree" or "wood" is a plant with roots, trunk, and branches (left). Ideographs represent abstract ideas such as "on" or "above" (right).

The long history of the Chinese language is tied to written books. As a result, many phrases from old documents have come into common usage. In their everyday spoken language, the Chinese use four-word phrases taken from ancient written works. "Fox Assumes Tiger's Might" is an example of one such phrase from the ancient book *Records of the Warring States*:

Fox Assumes Tiger's Might

A tiger caught a fox while looking for any beast that might come his way and fall prey to him.

"Don't you dare eat me!" said the fox. "The Emperor of Heaven has made me king of the beasts. You eat me and you will be going against his orders. If you don't believe what I say, just let me lead the way and you follow close behind. Then we'll see if they all flee or not at the sight of me."

The tiger agreed to the idea, and so the two of them set off together. When the other beasts saw them coming, they all turned tail. Not realizing it was he that was the cause of their panic-stricken flight, the tiger thought they were afraid of the fox.

A young schoolboy practicing traditional calligraphy using a brush

Classical Chinese is still taught in schools. But the vernacular, or everyday spoken Chinese, called *bai hua* is used for newspapers, books, and poetry in today's China. Bai hua replaced classical Chinese in the 1920s.

Despite the switch to bai hua, the complicated written system of Chinese meant that only those with a good education could read and write. The Communist government set out to teach every citizen of the People's Republic of China to read. They developed simplified versions of many characters.

During the Long March, each person had one important character written on the back of his or her jacket. The marchers were instructed to learn a new character each day by walking behind a different person. By the end of the Long March, each person knew several hundred Chinese characters. This was the foundation of literacy for governing the new state.

The system of pinyin was also developed to translate characters into a romanized version. Pinyin was used to teach China's minorities as well as foreigners.

Like most children in the West, the first thing a Chinese child learns to write is his or her name. Chinese names reflect the importance of the family unit in traditional Chinese society. A Chinese name begins with the family name. This reflects the view that the individual is defined by family membership. In Chinese society, individuality is less important than a person's ability to assume responsibilities within the family.

Most Chinese have family names from "The One Hundred Names." These are the Smiths, Browns, and Joneses of the Chinese-speaking world. Some common names in China are *Wang* (king), *Lee* (plum), *Zhang* (to draw a bow), and *Chen* (coin).

A person's family name is usually followed by two given names. In many cases, the first given name indicates a particular generation in that person's family. That character might come from a family poem. The second of the two given names often shows a special wish for the child. Boys' names might contain a reference to brilliance or luck. Or they might signal a responsibility to the ancestors. For girls, a flower name is often given to signify beauty or a feminine trait.

Chinese often have nicknames. Nicknames may be based on where they were born, a particular physical trait, or an accomplishment.

Xingming

Chinese use the word *xing* for a family name and *ming* for a person's given names. When asking a person's name, the Chinese say: "Your honorable family name?" A request for a person's full name would be: "Your xing/ming?"

The door of a house displaying two lines of verse in Chinese characters

Between Heaven and Earth

Much of the spiritual life in today's China is not tied to any major philosophy or religion. It is tied to Chinese mythology, world view, history, and legend.

C

Yin and Yang

HINESE WORLD VIEW CONSISTS OF TWO OPPOSING YET complementary forces—yin and yang. Yin is the female, passive, cool force. Yang is the male, active, hot source. These forces are engaged in an endless cycle of movement and change. This is best illustrated by the *taiji*. This never-ending cycle of peaks and valleys also expresses the Chinese view of life, history, and everything else in the world.

Buddhism, Islam, Christianity, and even Judaism all took root in China at one time or another. However, these were seen as foreign religions or philosophies, as opposed to the schools of Confucianism and Taoism, which are native Chinese philosophies.

Religion in the People's Republic of China is officially regarded as superstition. The Communist government embraces atheism. According to Communist theory, religion is a tool used by the ruling class to keep the workers happy in their misery.

Today, interest in religion is on the rise in officially atheist China, but it is strictly controlled. Mosques, temples, and churches must be approved by the government. This is done in order to keep people loyal to the People's Republic of China rather than to the pope in Rome, for example. Personal worship is free, but preaching outside the walls of approved religious centers is forbidden.

Opposite: **Buddha statues inside the South Putuo Temple in Xiamen**

Taiji

This symbol shows how each force contains some of its opposing force. As yang reaches its peak, it changes into yin. As the cycle continues and yin peaks, it changes into yang.

A monk arranging flowers by an altar in Tibet

Chinese Medicine

Each human being makes up a miniature universe in himself or herself. In Chinese medicine, illness is caused by an imbalance of yin and yang in the human body.

According to Chinese legend, Shen Nung, the legendary father of agriculture, tested China's various plants to discover their nutritional and medicinal properties. These plants are the basis for Chinese herbal medicine.

The Chinese prescribe a combination of herbs, brewed into a soup, to cure various illnesses. Peach pits and safflower, for example, are used to improve blood circulation. Ginseng is used to strengthen the heart. Cassia bark is used to treat colds.

Religion and Cultural Revolution

During the Cultural Revolution, temples, mosques, and churches across the country were destroyed. Buddhist monks, Muslim mullahs, and Christian priests and pastors were not allowed to practice their religion. Instead, they were sent into the countryside to work on the land and be "reeducated" in Communism.

Of all the religions and philosophies that came under attack during the Cultural Revolution, the teachings of Confucius, with their important political message, came under special attack. Confucianism was viewed as a symbol of the oppression of Imperial China.

A ritual celebration of Confucius's birthday

Confucianism

The sayings of the philosopher Confucius are recorded in *The Analects*. Confucian philosophy is not based on a heavenly philosophy. Instead, it is firmly based upon earthly life and the relationships between people.

Confucius taught that one never acts alone, but that one's actions affect others and must not create harm or tension. The correct way to rule, Confucius argued, is to set a moral example for the people to follow.

During the Han dynasty, Confucianism was adopted as the state philosophy. *The Analects* became the basis of all education in China. Confucianism was the basis for training government officials until the establishment of the Republic of China in 1912.

The ideas of obedience to parents and respect for elderly people and ritual were in direct conflict with Communist ideas. Nevertheless, the principles of the ancient philosopher are a defining source of Chinese culture and thinking. And Confucianism, with its emphasis on stability and respect for order and authority, has been used by the Communists as a tool to keep order.

Taoism

Taoism is a philosophy said to have been founded by Laozi. The *tao*, or the "way," at the center of the philosophy, is the ultimate reality and mystery of life. It is the driving force of

Religions of China*	
No religion	59%
Traditional Chinese religions (Confucianism, Taoism)	20%
Atheism	12%
Buddhism	6%
Islam	2%
Christianity	0.2%

*Does not total 100% due to rounding

nature and the idea behind the order of the universe and all life. It can never be exhausted.

Those who practice Taoism reject aggression, competition, and ambition. Humility and selflessness are thought to go hand in hand with the rejection of material goods, high rank, and social status. For Taoists, society is class-free and democratic. Because of this, Taoism is associated with political protest and rebellion. This brought the philosophy into conflict with the government of China.

Buddhism

Buddhism is not centered on a god, but on the attainment of *nirvana*, a condition beyond the limits of the mind and body. The Buddha wrote nothing, and books about his philosophy date from well after his death.

The Gold Hill Temple Buddhist ceremony

Buddhism is a religion that reached China from India. A rich prince named Siddhartha Gautama became discontented with the world when faced with the prospects of sickness, old age, and death. At the age of thirty, he gave up his worldly ties and began a search for enlightenment. He began with Hindu philosophy and yoga, became a hermit, and finally went on to meditation and mystic concentration. Buddhist legend recounts his achievement of enlightenment as he sat in meditation beneath a bodhi tree.

Carved Buddhas

Before Buddhism, sculpture representing spiritual or philosophical ideas was foreign to China. Afterward, a series of massive Buddhas, like those in India, began to appear on China's landscape. Some of the most famous of these carved Buddhas are in the caves at Lungmen and Yunggang.

At Dunhuang, along the Silk Routes, a series of caves carved into the cliffs and decorated with painted plaster have survived from China's Middle Ages. The subjects of these early frescoes are Jataka tales from the life of the Buddha. Drawing upon Indian legend and folklore, they tell of the Buddha's various forms during his many incarnations.

The Dalai Lama

The Dalai Lama is the spiritual leader of Tibetan Buddhism. There have been fourteen Dalai Lamas so far. The title *Dalai Lama* means "Ocean of Wisdom." Tibetan Buddhists believe that the present Dalai Lama is divine and that he will be reincarnated immediately upon his death. The present Dalai Lama lives in India. He left China in 1959 after the Tibetan revolt against Chinese Communists.

Between Heaven and Earth   **103**

Ping-Pong and Poetry

One of the most popular games among Chinese children is an import from the West. Almost every Chinese child plays ping-pong. Ping-pong originated in Britain, where it is called table tennis.

W HILE YOU MIGHT ROOT FOR A FAVORITE BASEBALL OR basketball team, Chinese kids follow ping-pong competition with tremendous enthusiasm. Chinese players sweep the Olympic field in the sport at each match.

Opposite: **Chinese opera**

Soccer is among China's most popular sports for both men and women. The world's first-ever women's soccer championship was held in China in 1991. During the 1996 Olympics held in Atlanta, Georgia, American women took the gold and Chinese women got the silver.

Badminton is popular with athletes throughout Asia. Olympic badminton matches feature shuttlecocks that travel 200 miles (322 km) per hour! During the 1996 Olympics, China's men's, women's, and doubles teams took home medals.

Richard Nixon's Visit to China

When China normalized political relations with the United States, one of the first steps in the process was a ping-pong match in Beijing. The Americans lost every game. But the ping-pong matches helped build the foundations of a new relationship between China and the United States.

President Richard Nixon's visit in 1972 was a direct result of this initial step involving ping-pong. The ping-pong ball ushered in a new political era and the lifting of the Bamboo Curtain. This became known as "ping-pong diplomacy."

Children in Beijing throwing paper airplanes

Games

Kites, tops, yo-yos, and POGS are popular games with children around the world. And they all have their roots in China.

Kites made of silk or paper stretched across a bamboo frame grew out of the native plants of China. Kites were tools in China before they were toys. Ancient Chinese used silk kites to communicate with heavenly spirits. They wrote messages asking for rain or good harvests on the kites and then released the kites to carry their messages to the heavens.

The Chinese realized that kites could be used for military purposes. Kites were flown to call troops to action. By constructing huge kites in the form of eagles, Chinese flew men above enemy troops to report on their movements.

Today, these military uses for kites are reflected in the Chinese sport of kite fighting. The competitors cover the line nearest the kite with ground glass or sand. Using the lines as saws, they try to cut their opponent's kite loose by engaging in a series of daring swoops, dodges, and quick darts.

When the Chinese invented paper during the Han dynasty (206 B.C.–A.D. 220), kite flying became an inexpensive amusement for everyone. Kite flying was integrated into folk festivals. Today, the skies over China are filled with colorful kites. The Chinese call kites *feng zhen* ("wind zither") because of the sound of the wind as it passes through holes in the kite's bamboo frame.

Children playing a popular Chinese board game called *Weiqi*, or Surround Chess. In North America, the game is known by the Japanese name of Go.

Tops have been found in prehistoric burials in China. A top may be made of bamboo, lotus seedpods, acorns, or conch shells, depending on the environment of the region.

A double top, spun side to side on a string stretched between two poles, is called a "diabolo" in the West. This top can be flipped in the air and caught on the string in order to keep it in constant motion.

Another kind of Chinese spinning toy is made of two disks of wood that travel up and down a string. In 1932, the Louis Toy Company copyrighted the name *yo-yo* and popularized the entertainment in the West.

Once paper became inexpensive, the Chinese manufactured a number of games made of paper. A folded paper toy is used in POGS, a game recently introduced in North America. In the Chinese version of POGS, the paper is folded into triangles. Each player tries to "whip" over the other players' pieces with his own POG.

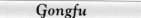

Stamp Collecting

The number-one hobby in today's China is stamp collecting. Both adults and children in China eagerly collect postage stamps from around the world. China's own postage stamps often feature scenic spots in China or historic events in the People's Republic of China. They are China's ambassadors of culture around the world.

A taijiquan master exercising

Gongfu

Perhaps the sport that Westerners most associate with the Chinese is *gongfu* (kung fu), a term that has entered the English language thanks to the late martial arts star Bruce Lee. Gongfu originated in China at the Shaolin Temple in Henan Province.

Today, gongfu includes boxing, weapon wielding, and different types of exercises used to promote good health. Gongfu styles are basically divided between northern and southern styles, and internal and external styles.

External gongfu exercises the body's tendons, bones, and skin. Many of the exercises are based on the movements of animals, such as the tiger, panther, monkey, snake, and crane. Internal gongfu trains the spirit and the mind. Each day, as dawn breaks, the streets begin to fill with Chinese gathering to perform the traditional exercises called *taijiquan* (t'ai chi ch'uan).

People participating in the traditional Chinese exercises of taijiquan at the wall of the Forbidden City

Acrobatics and Gymnastics

Balance, strength, flexibility, and grace are all found in Chinese acrobatics. Acrobatics include balancing and tumbling as well as juggling swords, balls, and pottery containers.

Chinese Olympic diver Fu Mingxu

The acrobatic troupe from Shanghai has toured the world to tremendous acclaim, acting as China's cultural ambassador.

During the 1998 Goodwill Games, the Chinese gymnast Sang Lan fell during a routine practice session. The young athlete suffered injuries that left her paralyzed from the neck down. Sang is being treated with a combination of cutting-edge Western sports medical techniques and traditional Chinese medicine.

Sang is confident she will walk and eventually compete again. She remains in extremely high spirits, capturing the interest and support of people around the world. Sang has received visits from international stars such as actor Leonardo DiCaprio and singer Celine Dion. Letters of encouragement have been sent to her by President Bill Clinton and former presidents Jimmy Carter and Ronald Reagan.

Chinese Opera

Acrobatics are important in the Chinese circus and are also featured in Chinese opera, a special form of theater. Opera is one of

An opera performer on stage dressed as the Monkey King in *Journey to the West,* a well-known Chinese tale

China's most popular entertainments. It became a celebrated form of amusement in Imperial China and has been beloved by both young and old for centuries.

As in imperial times, opera is often found in the market-place. For a few cents, shoppers can watch a performance while enjoying favorite Chinese snacks, such as dried squid or melon seeds, and sipping tea.

Masks

Each style of facial makeup in Chinese opera tells the audience about the personality of the character as well as his or her intentions. Red symbolizes loyalty and courage, while black represents a swashbuckling character. A character in blue makeup has a calculating nature, and white makeup tells the audience that this is a deceitful person whose trickery and dishonesty has an important role in the plot.

A "complete face" in Chinese opera is made up in a single and consistent manner. A "fragmented face" combines many elements. It may take many hours to paint a single character's face.

Operas are often based upon historical events. Stylized gestures, gymnastics, and elaborate makeup and costume are part of each performance. Opera performers begin training when they are very young in order to perform the necessary singing, recitation, eye movements, gestures, gymnastics, and movements. They spend years practicing and perfecting the elaborate makeup featured in each performance.

Film

Another cultural ambassador from China is Zhang Yimou, whose films have been seen by millions around the world. Zhang's films are based on the lives of ordinary Chinese men and women. His films show how social conditions and historical events affect their lives.

Many of Zhang's films focus on the lives of Chinese women before they were granted equal rights by the Communist government. *Raise the Red Lantern* tells the story of a powerful man with many wives. *Shanghai Triad* shows the corruption of that city before the founding of the People's Republic of China. But Zhang is sometimes critical of the government, showing, for example, the harsh realities of China's Cultural Revolution in his film *To Live*. The actress Gong Li stars in many of his films.

The director Xie Fei is also beginning to receive international recognition for his films. A graduate of—and now a professor at—Beijing Film College, Xie has based most of his films on twentieth-century Chinese novels.

Our Fields, Xie's first independently directed film, shows the lives of a group of urban teenagers during the Cultural Revolution. The film also depicts their lives in the countryside. *The Year of Bad Luck*, a tragic tale about a young city dweller, won the Silver Bear award at the Berlin International Film Festival in 1990.

Xie's films always emphasize the inner life of his subjects. "The topics of my films differ from one another," explains Xie, "but kindness and human nature will never change.

Television

Television in China is controlled by the government. During President Clinton's 1998 state visit, Clinton and Chinese president Jiang Zemin exchanged political views. The two leaders engaged in a spirited debate about human rights, government, and the future of the United States and China. China Central Television, the state network, broadcast the debate live. It was estimated that 600 million Chinese watched the debate on television.

China's most popular television show is entitled *A Beijinger in New York*. It tells the story of a young musician who emigrates to the United States. A professional cellist in China, the musician is unable to find work in New York. He spends his days working in Chinese restaurants and sweatshops in Chinatown.

Popular Music

The theme of *A Beijinger in New York* has been recorded by Liu Huan, one of China's most famous pop artists. A teacher by profession, Liu has recorded a number of popular songs.

Xiao Nan is singer and guitarist for a Chinese rock band.

Cui Jian is China's most famous rock star. Admired by many young Chinese, Cui's songs express his dissatisfaction with today's China. Cui's most famous song is "I Have Nothing." Cui represents the first generation of Chinese rock artists. Previously, young Chinese were greatly influenced by rock stars from Hong Kong.

The Three Perfections

The arts of calligraphy, poetry, and painting are called the "Three Perfections" in China. From the Song dynasty (960–1279) onward, the practice of the Three Perfections was viewed as the mark of an educated person.

All educated men and women were participants in this artistic tradition. As a result, more people practice these arts in China than in the West.

The Chinese feel that the combination of calligraphy, poetry, and painting is the height of artistic expression. And since these three arts are all arts of the brush, the Chinese often combine them on a single work.

Painting

Western art often concerns itself with the human body and human emotions. The Chinese feel that human life is just a small part of the universe. Chinese art is more concerned with nature and the workings of the universe.

The Chinese view the universe as composed of two forces—yin and yang. Yin, the female force is cool and passive. It is best represented by water. Yang, the male force, is hot and active. It is best represented by rocks and mountains.

A Small Neighborhood in Suzhou by Xu Xi

By painting a landscape composed of these two elements, the Chinese portray a universe that is in both balance and continual change. The Chinese use the term *shanshui*, literally "mountains/water," for such works. So a landscape painting for the Chinese is not just a picture of scenery, but a statement about an orderly world where all elements are in balance.

Chinese paintings often include inscriptions. These might be a dedication of the painting to a friend, an explanation of why and when the work was done, or a poem related to the subject of the painting. For example, one scholar could paint a landscape. Another would write a line of poetry on the painting. A third might add an inscription describing the circumstances under which the work was done.

Over the years, other scholars would add comments of appreciation for the work. The Chinese felt that viewing such a work and adding a fresh inscription allowed scholars to commune intellectually over the years and miles that separated them, and allowed a painting to grow. So what might be considered graffiti by Westerners is actually highly esteemed by the Chinese.

In Communist China, calligraphy by famous politicians might be added to a painting. One famous example of this is Mao's calligraphy on a seemingly limitless landscape of rivers and mountains.

In contemporary China, artists have added new dimensions and aspects to traditional Chinese forms by acquiring Western techniques and theory. Nevertheless, the traditional combination of image and word is still an effective force of personal communication.

A seventeenth-century blue-and-white Chinese porcelain piece designed for export to the West

A young girl in calligraphy class at the Children's Palace, Shanghai

For the Chinese, writing is a way of communicating many things. Chinese people don't just read the words, they look at the way the words are written. They believe that a person's handwriting is like a fingerprint of his or her thoughts.

This attitude toward handwriting developed with the invention of paper during the Han dynasty. The highly absorbent paper allowed the reader to see every movement of the hand that wrote the complex Chinese characters. Nothing could be hidden, erased, or corrected. Likewise, the Chinese felt, the written character revealed the person's inner character. For these reasons, Chinese considered calligraphy to be the highest art form, valuing the written word over painting as an artist's innermost expression.

A bold and balanced handwriting meant the person was courageous and moderate. Sloppy, weak characters indicated a lazy mind that was not dependable.

Chinese poetry uses the unique character of the Chinese language. Because Chinese is basically a language of one-syllable words, the Chinese have added tones to make different words. Chinese poems need to rhyme as well as to be balanced in tone. In addition, the physical composition of Chinese words must also be balanced.

Night Thoughts

A poem by Li Po called "Night Thoughts" demonstrates the five-character poetry of the Tang dynasty. The Chinese characters next to the English translation illustrate the balanced qualities of the poem.

李白 (Li Po)

*The bright moon shone
before my bed,*

床 前 明 月 光

*I wondered —
was it frost upon the ground?*

疑 是 地 上 霜

*I raised my head
to gaze at the clear moon,*

舉 頭 望 明 月

*Bowed my head
remembering my old home.*

低 頭 思 故 鄉

The Future of the World

Officially, every man, woman, and child in the People's Republic of China works on Beijing time. The idea is that the government and its bureaucrats are always working together across China's several time zones for the future of the country.

120

I N REALITY, IT IS NOT BEIJING OFFICIALS, BUT THE RISING SUN that governs China's days. For thousands of years, Chinese farmers have awakened at dawn in order to start their day before the sun made work too difficult. Today, in a population where eight out of ten people are engaged in farming, the dawn still signals the start of China's day.

All Chinese children are assigned community responsibilities. If you lived in the city, after washing and dressing, you might sweep the streets. If you lived in the country, like most Chinese children, you would do some farm chores such as feeding the chickens.

Opposite: **A young man ready for a Chinese New Year parade**

Breakfast is eaten before setting out for work or school. In the north, breakfast is usually noodles or bread made of wheat flour. Southern children often eat a rice porridge called *congee,* topped with shrimp, vegetables, or pickles. They might also enjoy a glass of soybean milk, hot or cold, to which either sugar or soy sauce has been added.

Oil Stick and Sesame Bread

One of the favorite breakfast treats in China is a fried bread sandwich! A soft-baked roll topped with sesame seeds is used to hold a piece of deep-fried dough called an oil stick. Many vendors on the streets of China's cities sell this treat.

The Future of the World **121**

A man eating with chopsticks at the market in Datong

Chinese use chopsticks and a spoon to eat their meals. The Western custom of using a knife at the table is looked upon with distaste. Chinese feel that knives should be used in the kitchen, but not at the table.

Chinese cooking methods show how a cook can make the most of the flavors of the ingredients using a minimum of fuel. Foods are chopped into small pieces and quick-cooked. Chinese often stir-fry their foods in a pan called a wok. This is a frying pan with a curved bottom. A little oil is used to coat the surface of the pan, and the food is moved quickly in the pan.

Steaming is another popular method for Chinese cooking. Using bamboo, the Chinese use flat-bottomed baskets that can be stacked on top of one another. Each basket is lined with a cabbage leaf and the food placed inside. The stacked baskets are then placed over a pan of boiling water and the food is cooked.

Dumplings

Dumplings are a popular snack for the Chinese, filled with meat, fish, or vegetables. The dumplings may be boiled, steamed, or fried. This recipe is for fried dumplings, *guo tieh*, literally called "potstickers."

Potstickers:

2 1/2 cups of all-purpose wheat flour

2/3 cup boiling water

2/3 cup cold water

3/4 lb. ground pork

4 oz. shelled shrimp, minced

3 dried black mushrooms (soaked and minced)

1 T chopped scallion

1 t ginger

2 T soy sauce

2 t salt

2 t sesame oil or lard

10 oz. cabbage (bok choy is best)

3 T oil

1. Add boiling water to flour, mix with chopsticks, then add cold water, and knead it very well. Let stand for at least 15 minutes covered with cloth.

2. Place pork in bowl, add minced shrimp, minced mushrooms, scallion, ginger, soy sauce, salt, sesame oil or lard. Mix thoroughly until thickened.

3. Cook cabbage in boiling water about 2 minutes. Plunge in cold water and squeeze dry before chopping finely. Add to mixture from step 2.

4. Remove dough to floured board and knead again until smooth. Divide the dough into 40 pieces. Flatten each piece by hand and roll into 2 1/2" diameter thin pancake. Put 1 tablespoon of filling from step 3 in center, fold over to make a half-circle, and pinch edges together.

5. Heat a flat frying pan until very hot, add 2 tablespoons oil. Add dumplings to cover bottom of pan without overlapping. Fry until bottom is golden (about one minute). Add 2/3 cup water, cover, and cook until water has evaporated.

6. Add 1 tablespoon oil to side of pan and fry another half-minute. Place a serving plate over the frying pan and invert the pan quickly. Now prepare the remaining portions.

A street in Beijing during rush hour

In the People's Republic of China, breakfast, like other meals, is cooked on a stove shared by many families. China's population crunch means that kitchens, bathrooms, and laundry facilities are often shared by several families. In the cities, a family might live in housing built by and for members of their *danwei* (work unit). Many Chinese live and work with the same people day in and day out.

As the workday begins, China's roads turn into a river of spinning bicycle wheels. Couples often travel on a single bicycle with their one child. The child is securely fastened in a bamboo seat.

Chinese children go to school six days a week. Throughout China, it is the duty of each class to keep its own classroom clean and tidy. The school day begins at 8:30 in the morning. Before classes, the entire school assembles for ten minutes of exercise.

Because there is a shortage of both teachers and classroom space in China, classes are large and crowded. Since each family has only one child, there is a great deal of pressure to succeed in school. Children are taught to listen carefully to the teacher.

The goal of China's educational system is to produce citizens who can help rebuild the country. Engineers and scientists are greatly needed. Also, the country is training students in business to help rebuild the country's economy and attract foreign investment.

Young Pioneers

The goal of every child is to do well in school and be recommended for the Young Pioneers. Much like Boy Scouts and Girl Scouts, Young Pioneers are encouraged to develop self-reliance.

In China, Young Pioneers represent the ideal Communist characteristics of bravery, initiative, and self-sacrifice. Children in the Pioneers wear red neckerchiefs to symbolize the Communist future of their country. They often represent their class at school ceremonies.

Kindergarten children attending class in Shanghai

National Holidays in the People's Republic of China

New Year's Day	January 1
Spring Festival (Chinese New Year)	Date varies
International Working Women's Day	March 8
International Labor Day	May 1
Youth Day	May 4
Children's Day	June 1
Founding of the Communist Party of China Day	July 1
Founding of the People's Liberation Army Day	August 1
Teachers' Day	September 10
National Day	October 1–2

Children attend elementary school for six years. Middle school lasts from three to six years depending upon the course of study. At present, college and graduate schools are only a dream for many Chinese children. Competition for admission is extremely difficult.

Children eat lunch at noon. This is followed by a rest from one to two o'clock. Don't forget, the children have been awake since early morning!

Free time in the schoolyard is a favorite time for Chinese children, just as it is for children around the world. Many of the games played by Chinese children would be familiar to you. But some games date back thousands of years in Chinese culture.

Jianzi is a sport similar to badminton but it uses no racquets. It uses a shuttlecock. The object of the game is to keep the shuttlecock in the air by catching it on the sole or heel of the foot. Chinese children often make their own shuttlecock by wrapping a bit of rag or soft leather around an old-style Chinese coin with a hole in the middle. Goose quills are poked through the central hole to help keep the shuttlecock in the air.

Once school is over at 4:30, many children head to an after-school program at the local Children's Palace. Here,

groups of children join together to sing and dance, do some artwork, or play games until their parents' workday is finished.

When the family meets for dinner, parents and children are often joined by grandparents, cousins, aunts, and uncles. Dinner, homework, and bed are the usual order of the day. By nine o'clock, most parents and children are in bed, ready to get up at dawn the next day.

All Chinese children know that they are the new generation of the world's oldest continuous civilization. But they also understand that they are citizens of the world's most populous nation and emerging superpower.

Schoolchildren on an outing to the Summer Palace in Beijing

Timeline

China's History

The Yangshao culture reaches its peak in the Huanghe Valley.	About 3000 B.C.
The Shang establish China's first dynasty.	About 1766 B.C.
The Zhou dynasty rules China.	1059–221 B.C.
The great Chinese philosopher Confucius lives.	551–479 B.C.
The Chinese Empire is formed under the Qin dynasty; building of the Great Wall begins.	221-206 B.C.
The Han dynasty rules China.	206 B.C.–A.D. 220
The Chinese Empire is divided during the Period of Disunity.	A.D. 220–581
The Sui dynasty reunites the Chinese Empire and begins building the Grand Canal.	581–618
The Tang dynasty rules the empire.	618–907
Five dynasties and ten kingdoms struggle to control China.	907–960
The Song dynasty reunifies China.	960–1279
Mongol leader Kublai Khan defeats the Song and establishes the Yuan dynasty with Beijing as the Chinese capital.	1279–1368
The Ming overthrow the Mongols and establish their own dynasty.	1368–1644

World History

c. 2500 B.C.	Egyptians build the Pyramids and Sphinx in Giza.
563 B.C.	Buddha is born in India.
A.D. 313	The Roman emperor Constantine recognizes Christianity.
610	The prophet Muhammad begins preaching a new religion called Islam.
1054	The Eastern (Orthodox) and Western (Roman) Churches break apart.
1066	William the Conqueror defeats the English in the Battle of Hastings.
1095	Pope Urban II proclaims the First Crusade.
1215	King John seals the Magna Carta.
1300s	The Renaissance begins in Italy.
1347	The Black Death sweeps through Europe.
1453	Ottoman Turks capture Constantinople, conquering the Byzantine Empire.
1492	Columbus arrives in North America.
1500s	The Reformation leads to the birth of Protestantism.

China's History

The Manchu overthrow the Ming and rule China as the Qing dynasty.	1644–1911
The Treaty of Nanjing gives Hong Kong to Britain.	1842
Chinese revolutionaries overthrow the Qing dynasty.	1911
Sun Yat-sen becomes president of the Chinese Republic.	1912
The Chinese Communist Party is founded.	1921
Chiang Kai-shek sets up the Nationalist government in Nanjing.	1927
Chinese Nationalists and Communists fight a civil war.	1946–1949
Communist Party Chairman Mao Zedong declares the formation of the People's Republic of China; Chiang Kai-shek's Nationalist forces retreat to Taiwan and set up the Republic of China.	1949
Mao Zedong begins the Great Leap Forward.	1958
Mao Zedong begins the Cultural Revolution.	1966
The People's Republic of China is admitted to the United Nations.	1971
Mao Zedong dies.	1976
China's Communist Party moves toward less government control of the economy under Deng Xiaoping.	1980s
Student protesters against government corruption are killed by the military in Beijing's Tiananmen Square.	1989
Deng Xiaoping dies; Great Britain returns control of Hong Kong to China.	1997

World History

1776	The Declaration of Independence is signed.
1789	The French Revolution begins.
1865	The American Civil War ends.
1914	World War I breaks out.
1917	The Bolshevik Revolution brings Communism to Russia.
1929	Worldwide economic depression begins.
1939	World War II begins, following the German invasion of Poland.
1957	The Vietnam War starts.
1989	The Berlin Wall is torn down, as Communism crumbles in Eastern Europe.
1996	Bill Clinton re-elected U.S. president.

Fast Facts

Official name: People's Republic of China

Capital: Beijing

Official language: Mandarin Chinese

Qomolangma

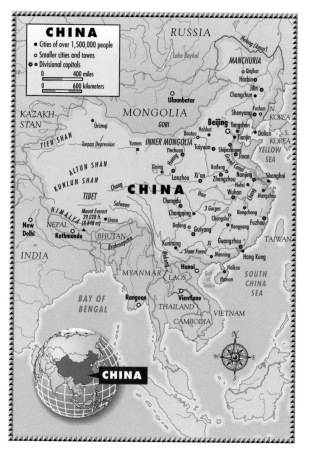

Flag of the People's Republic
of China

Calligraphy class

Official religion: None

National anthem: "March of the Volunteers"

Government: One-party government with one legislative house

Chief of state: President

Head of government: Premier

Area: 3,696,100 square miles (9,572,160 sq km)

**Coordinates of
geographic center:** 34° 15' N, 109° 0' E

Bordering countries: The People's Republic of China is bordered by
Russia to the north and east; Mongolia to the
north; Kazakhstan, Kyrgyzstan, Tajikistan,
Afghanistan, and Pakistan to the west; India,
Nepal, Bhutan, Myanmar (Burma), Laos, Vietnam,
and the South China Sea to the south; and North
Korea, the Yellow Sea, and the East China Sea to
the east.

Highest elevation: *Qomolangma* (Mount Everest), 29,028 feet (8,848 m)

Lowest elevation: Turpan Depression in Xinjiang, 505 feet (154 m)
below sea level

Average temperatures: Lowest: –22°F (–30°C) in January in northern
China
Highest: 83°F (28°C) in July in southeastern China

**Average annual
rainfall:** Northwestern deserts: less than 4 inches (10 cm)
Southeastern coast: 60–80 inches (150–200 cm)

**National population
(1997 est.):** 1,210,004,956

Shanghai

The Great Wall

Currency

Population of largest cities (1995 est.):

Shanghai	13,584,000
Beijing	11,299,000
Tianjin	9,415,000
Shenyang	5,116,000
Guangzhou	4,492,000

Famous landmarks:

▶ *Great Wall* (northern China, especially in the area of Badaling)

▶ *Forbidden City* (Beijing)

▶ *Lishan Mausoleum* (Shaanxi Province)

▶ *Three Gorges* (Sichuan-Hubei border)

▶ *Stone Forest* (Yunnan Province)

▶ *Big Goose Pagoda* (Xian, Shaanxi Province)

Industry: China's major industries are the manufacture of machinery, transportation equipment, and steel. Producing chemicals such as plastics and medicines is the country's second-largest industry. Textiles, food processing, and clothing are also important. Although light industry that produces consumer goods is growing, heavy industry still leads China's manufactured goods.

Currency: The *Renminbi* ("People's Money"), also called the *yuan* (Y); 1999 exchange rate: U.S.$1 = 8.28Y

Weights and measures: Metric system for international trade; Chinese system for internal activities: 1 *chi* = 1.0936 feet; 1 *mu* = 0.1644 acres; 1 *jin* = 1.1023 pounds

Literacy rate: 81.5% (1994)

The Summer Palace, Beijing

Deng Xiaoping

Common Chinese words and phrases:

baifan (buy-fahn)	rice
Bu xie (buu she-eh)	you're welcome
cha (chah)	tea
ganbu (gahn-buu)	an administrator in the Chinese Communist Party
guo tieh (gwaw tee-eh)	a crispy brown dumpling
jianzi (jee-in-dzu)	a game played with a shuttlecock
kuaizi (kwie-dzu)	chopsticks
ni hao (nee how)	hello
qing (cheeng)	please
xie xie (she-eh she-eh)	thank you
zai-jian (zigh-jee-in)	good-bye
…zai nar? (zigh nah-urr)	Where is . . .?
Zhe shi duo shao? (juh shr dwaw shah-oh)	How much is this?

Famous people:

Confucius *Philosopher*	(551–479 B.C.)
Deng Xiaoping *Communist leader*	(1904–1997)
Jiang Zemin *President*	(1926–)
Li Po *Poet*	(701–762)
Mao Zedong *Communist leader*	(1893–1976)
Zhang Yimou *Filmmaker*	(1950–)

To Find Out More

Nonfiction

▶ Blunden, Caroline, and Mark Elvin. *Cultural Atlas of China*. Oxford: Phaidon Press, 1983.

▶ Clunas, Craig. *Art in China*. New York: Oxford University Press, 1997.

▶ Cotterell, Arthur. *Ancient China*. New York: Alfred A. Knopf, 1994.

▶ Dramer, Kim. *Games People Play: China*. Danbury, Conn.: Children's Press, 1997.

▶ Hook, Brian, ed. *The Cambridge Encyclopedia of China*. Cambridge: Cambridge University Press, 1991.

Websites

▶ **Asia Society**
http://www.asiasociety.org/
Official website for the Asia Society, a nonprofit, nonpartisan educational institution dedicated to fostering an understanding between Asians and Americans.

▶ **Asian Reading Room of the Library of Congress**
http://lcweb.loc.gov/rr/asian
Represents one of the largest collections of Asian-language materials in the world. Includes legal materials, films, manuscripts, maps, music, and photographs from Southeast Asia to China, Japan, and Korea.

▶ **Ask Asia**

http://www.askasia.org/

Offers easy access to high-quality, classroom-tested resources and cultural information, engaging games and activities, and links to relevant people, places, and institutions.

▶ **Ethnomusicology OnLine**

http://research.umbc.edu/eol

A peer-reviewed multimedia journal. Includes reviews of videos, books, CDs, and articles from a variety of ethnic groups.

Organizations and Embassies

▶ **Consulate-General of the People's Republic of China in New York**

520 12th Avenue

New York, NY 10036

Tel: (212) 868-7752

Fax: (212) 502-0245

E-mail: http://www.nyconsulate. prchina.org

▶ **Embassy of the People's Republic of China**

2201 Wisconsin Avenue, N.W.

Washington, DC 20007

Tel: (202) 338-6688

Fax: (202) 588-9760

E-mail: http://www.china-embassy.org/

▶ **National Tourism Administration of the People's Republic of China**

9A, Jianguomennei Dajie,

Beijing 100740

Tel: (010) 65201114

Telex: 210449 CNTA

Fax: (010) 65122096

E-mail: http://www.tiglion.com/ travel/china/touradmi.htm

Index

Page numbers in *italics* indicate illustrations.

Lee, Bruce, 108
legalism, 45–46
Lhasa apso (dog), 41
Li Po, 119, 133
Lishan Mausoleum, *12*
literacy, 96
literature, 87
Little Red Book, 61
loess silt, 23
long (dragon), 28–29, *29*
Long March, 56, 58, *58*, 96
Longevity Hill, 8
Lu Yu Lu, 34, 133

M

Manchurian tigers, 36
Mandarin Chinese (language), 87, 94
"Mandate of Heaven," 11
manufacturing, 18, 72, 76, 78–79, *82*
Mao Zedong, 55, *55*, 58, 60, *62*,
    65, 77, 133
maps
    agricultural, *75*
    Beijing, *73*
    geopolitical, *10*
    Han dynasty, *46*
    historical, *49*
    internal divisions, *22*
    land usage, *75*
    language regions, *94*
    mineral resources, *81*
    Ming dynasty, *49*
    Mongolian Empire, *49*
    population distribution, *87*
    Qing dynasty, *49*
    Silk Routes, *49*

topographical, *21*
    Treaty Ports, *51*
May Fourth Movement, 54–56
Middle Kingdom, 8, 13
military, 62–63, 68–70, *69*
    kite flying and, 106–107
    National Revolutionary Army, 57
millet farming, 76
mineral resources map, *81*
ming (given name), 97
Ming dynasty, 16, 49–50
    map of, *49*
mining, 79, 81
    mineral resources map, *81*
Mongolia, 89
    Inner Mongolia, 90
    Outer Mongolia, 90
    sports, 90
Mongolian Empire, 48–49
    map of, *49*
    Mongols, 48–49, 89
Mount Everest (*Qomolangma*),
    17, *17*, 20
mulberry trees, 38
music, 91, 114–115, *114*

N

Nadam Fair, 90
names, 96–97. *See also* nicknames.
Nanjing, 60
National Day Parade, 69
national emblem, 71
national flag, 71, *71*
national holidays, 126
National People's Congress (NPC),
    66, 67
National Revolutionary Army, 57

Nationalist Party, 57
nature reserves, 36
New Year's Day celebration, *29*, *120*
nicknames, 97. *See also* names.
Night Thoughts (poem), 119
Nixon, Richard, 61–62, *62*, 105
Northern Mongolia, 90

O

oil industry, 27
Olympic Games, 105, *110*
"One Child Only" campaign, 75, *75*
"The One Hundred Names," 97
opera, *104*, 110–112, *111*, *112*
Opium Wars, 50–51, *50*, 63
Our Fields (film), 113
Outer China, 15, 17, 19, 21–22, 35
Outer Mongolia, 90

P

peony (national flower), 32, *32*
people, 64, 86, 96, *106*, *118*, *125*,
    127. *See also* Famous people.
    Dai, 92, *92*
    education, 93, 96, *118*, 125–126,
    125, *127*
    elderly, 93, *93*
    filial piety (respect for elders), 93
    Han Chinese, 87, 91
    housing, 97
    literacy, 96
    median ages, 93
    minorities, 87
    Mongols, 48–49, 89
    names, 96–97
    population control, 75, *75*

Meet the Author

KIM DRAMER is a Ph.D. candidate in ancient Chinese art and architecture in the Department of Art History and Archaeology at Columbia University. She is currently writing her doctoral thesis on mortuary art of the Han dynasty.

Writing this book for the Enchantment of the World series, she used the libraries at Columbia University, including the Starr East Asian Library. This is one of the finest collections of scholarly books on China in the world. She also relied on her own personal trips to China, where she has traveled extensively, including a trip across the Gobi Desert along the ancient Silk Routes. She is pictured (opposite) in front of the Big Goose Pagoda in Xian.

Kim is the mother of twins, Alexandra and Max Wang— Wang Xiantang and Wang Xianhan. She is especially interested in writing for young adults to help improve the understanding between China and the West.

Photo Credits